DK HANDBOOKS
DINOSAURS
AND OTHER PREHISTORIC LIFE

SMITHSONIAN HANDBOOKS

DINOSAURS
AND OTHER PREHISTORIC LIFE

HAZEL RICHARDSON

Consultant
DR. GREGORY F. FUNSTON

NEW EDITION

DK DELHI

Senior Editor Suefa Lee
Senior Art Editor Mahua Sharma
Assistant Editor Nayan Keshan
Assistant Art Editors George Thomas, Aarushi Dhawan
DTP Designers Umesh Singh Rawat, Vijay Kandwal
Senior Managing Editor Rohan Sinha
Managing Art Editor Sudakshina Basu
Production Manager Pankaj Sharma
Pre-production Manager Sunil Sharma

DK LONDON

Editor Annie Moss
US Editors Kayla Dugger, Lori Hand
Managing Editor Angeles Gavira Guerrero
Managing Art Editor Michael Duffy
Jacket Design Development Manager Sophia MTT
Senior Production Controller Meskerem Berhane
Production Editor George Nimmo
Associate Publishing Director Liz Wheeler
Publishing Director Jonathan Metcalf
Art Director Karen Self

Consultant Dr. Gregory F. Funston

FIRST EDITION

Project Editor Cathy Meeus
Picture Researcher Mariana Sonnenberg
DTP Designer Rajan Shah
Senior Editor Angeles Gavira
Managing Editor Liz Wheeler

Art Editor Lee Riches
Designers Tracy Miles, Rebecca Milner
Production Controller Melanie Dowland
Senior Art Editor Ina Stradins
Managing Art Editor Phil Ormerod

Consultant Dr. David Norman

2/3D Digital illustrations Jon Hughes
Additional 3D content Russell Gooday

This American Edition, 2021
First American Edition, 2003
Published in the United States by DK Publishing
1450 Broadway, Suite 801, New York, NY 10018

A catalog record for this book is available from the Library of Congress.
ISBN 978-0-7440-2838-6

Printed and bound in China

For the curious
www.dk.com

Contents

HOW THIS BOOK WORKS

This book opens with an introductory section that describes the evolution of early animals, followed by a summary of the environment on Earth during its early history. The main part of the book contains profiles of the major prehistoric animals from the Mesozoic and Cenozoic Eras.

a map and description of the positions of the continents during each time period

introduction to prehistoric life for each time period

▲ The time periods

Each geological period is introduced in a double-page feature, detailing the climatic conditions and, where relevant, plant life and prevalent animal forms. A timeline at the bottom of the pages indicates the chronological position of the period.

species name

syllable-by-syllable pronunciation guide

the name of the paleontologist who first described the species, and the year in which the findings were published

habitat in which the animal lived

THEROPODS

e transition osystems, seudosuchians the early ds, became e ceratosaurs ated the food ge spawned the d top predators e until the . Tetanurans th some groups ts and horns, and others an elongated snout–taken to an extreme in the bizarre spinosaurs.

As these lineages were getting bigger, other groups like the coelurosaurs were

getting smaller, so theropods occupied a wide variety of ecological roles. Many of the lineages that would come to rule the Cretaceous originated in the Jurassic, including dromaeosaurs, tyrannosaurs, and troodontids. Some of these coelurosaurs, which were fast runners with relatively long arms, started to use their feathered forelimbs in unique ways, experimenting with generating lift by flapping or gliding. It is now clear that active powered flight originated independently multiple times in these dinosaurs, but one particular dinosaur, *Archaeopteryx* (see pp.70–71), was especially adept at flying. Its relatives continue to rule the skies today.

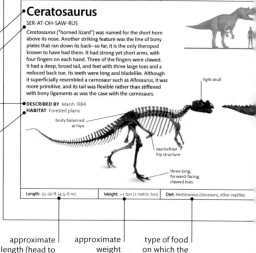

Group: THEROPODA	Subgroup: Ceratosauria	Time: 156–149 mya

Ceratosaurus
SER-AT-OH-SAW-RUS

Ceratosaurus ("horned lizard") was named for the short horn above its nose. Another striking feature was the line of bony plates that ran down its back–so far, it is the only theropod known to have had them. It had strong yet short arms, with four fingers on each hand. Three of the fingers were clawed. It had a deep, broad tail, and feet with three large toes and a reduced back toe. Its teeth were long and bladelike. Although it superficially resembled a carnosaur such as *Allosaurus*, it was more primitive, and its tail was flexible rather than stiffened with bony ligaments as was the case with the carnosaurs.

● **DESCRIBED BY** Marsh 1884
■ **HABITAT** Forested plains

light skull

body balanced at hips

saurischian hip structure

three long, forward-facing, clawed toes

Length: 15–20 ft (4.5–6 m)	Weight: ~1 ton (1 metric ton)	Diet: Herbivorous dinosaurs, other reptiles

approximate length (head to tail) or height

approximate weight

type of food on which the animal lived

▼ Animal profiles

Arranged by time period and by group, each major animal is described in detail. The text includes information about the animal's physical features, diet, and lifestyle. Colored bands summarize key information about classification, dates, dimensions, and diet. Each animal is illustrated by an artist's reconstruction and/or fossil remains. Key features are annotated. In each case a map identifies the approximate location of main fossil finds of that creature.

COLOR KEY

The bands at the top of each entry are color-coded to identify the time period to which it belongs.

Time-Period colors

	Precambrian		Triassic
	Cambrian		Jurassic
	Ordovician		Cretaceous
	Silurian		Paleogene
	Devonian		Neogene
	Carboniferous		Quaternary
	Permian		

scientific name of main group

scientific name of subgroup

time when the animal existed in millions of years ago (mya) or years ago (ya)

Theropods | 61

| Group: THEROPODA | Subgroup: Dilophosauridae | Time: 199–182 mya |

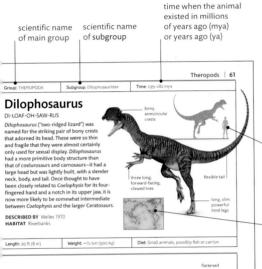

Dilophosaurus
DI-LOAF-OH-SAW-RUS

Dilophosaurus ("two-ridged lizard") was named for the striking pair of bony crests that adorned its head. These were so thin and fragile that they were almost certainly only used for sexual display. *Dilophosaurus* had a more primitive body structure than that of coelurosaurs and carnosaurs–it had a large head but was lightly built, with a slender neck, body, and tail. Once thought to have been closely related to *Coelophysis* for its four-fingered hand and a notch in its upper jaw, it is now more likely to be somewhat intermediate between *Coelophysis* and the larger Ceratosaurs.

DESCRIBED BY Welles 1970
HABITAT Riverbanks

bony, semicircular crests

three long, forward-facing, clawed toes

flexible tail

long, slim, powerful hind legs

the length or height of each animal is indicated in comparison to human dimensions

8 in (20 cm)

6 ft (1.8 m)

red dots indicate the location of principal fossil finds

| Length: 20 ft (6 m) | Weight: ~½ ton (500 kg) | Diet: Small animals, possibly fish or carrion |

▼ Feature spread

Animals of special interest are featured in a double-page entry. These show the animal in the type of landscape in which it is believed to have lived. Additional photographs and information boxes expand on the standard information for each featured animal.

flattened snout horn

bony plates running along back

long, flexible tail

long, powerful hind legs

long foot

reduced back toe

four-fingered h

artist's reconstruction gives an impression of the animal's appearance. Where fossil evidence is lacking, the interpretation is based on what is known about similar animals

CLASSIFICATION OF LIFE

AN ACCURATE UNDERSTANDING of living things and how they have evolved relies on their being classified into groups according to their similarity. Animals are classified in groups of decreasing diversity. The diagram outlines the evolution of the major groups of amniotes through time, from the diapsids and dinosaurs to the mammals. This is based on an analysis of shared features between species and their ancestors.

MONOPHYLETIC GROUPS

A monophyletic group is one that includes all the descendants of a common ancestor. This is in contrast to a paraphyletic group, where some descendants are left out, or a polyphyletic group, which artificially groups lineages that are not closely related. For example, dinosaurs are a monophyletic group only when birds—their direct descendants—are included. Paleontologists sometimes use paraphyletic groups, such as "nonavian dinosaurs," for convenience, but with the understanding that these are not meaningful evolutionary groupings. In this book, the Jurassic and Cretaceous "Other Diapsid" sections are paraphyletic groupings because they do not include dinosaurs.

KEY TO FOSSIL EVIDENCE

- Dinosaurs
- Pterosaurs
- Phytosaurs
- Pseudosuchians
- Rhynchosaurs
- Squamates
- Tanystropheids
- Ichthyopterygian
- Sauropterygians
- Diapsids
- Parareptiles
- Synapsids

NESTED CLADES

Paleontologists represent the relationships between animals using cladograms, where lineages are represented by branches joined at nodes to show common ancestry. Each node corresponds to a clade and can be given a formal name. These clades can also be joined to each other to show broader groups. This means that a species can be part of many nested clades of broader and broader membership—similar to the old Linnaean System, but with more levels. Paleontologists still use Linnaean names for genera and species, but most prefer to use nested clades instead of Linnaean ranks when discussing broader groups.

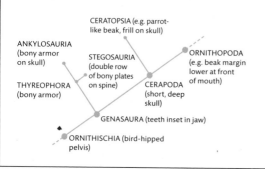

CERATOPSIA (e.g. parrot-like beak, frill on skull)

ANKYLOSAURIA (bony armor on skull)

STEGOSAURIA (double row of bony plates on spine)

ORNITHOPODA (e.g. beak margin lower at front of mouth)

THYREOPHORA (bony armor)

CERAPODA (short, deep skull)

GENASAURA (teeth inset in jaw)

ORNITHISCHIA (bird-hipped pelvis)

Archosauromorphs

Lepidosaurs

Diapsids

Parareptiles

Amniotes

PALEOZOIC

| Devonian 419–359mya | Carboniferous 359–299mya | Permian 299–252mya |

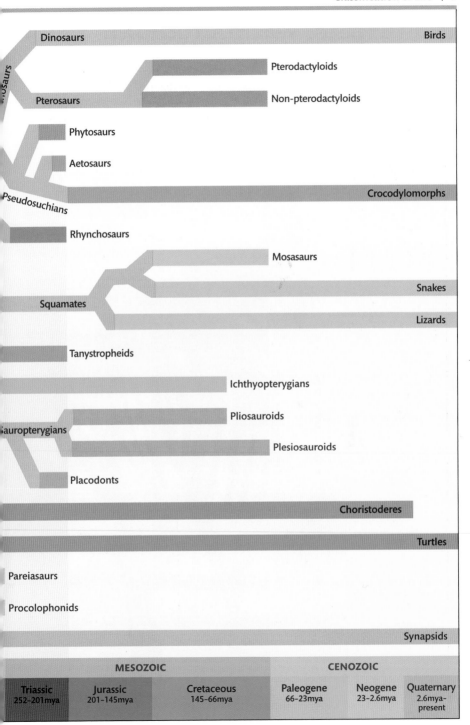

WHAT WERE DINOSAURS?

DINOSAURS DOMINATED the Earth's ecosystems for 165 million years. Although they evolved from a group of reptiles called the archosaurs, they possessed certain advanced features, as did other nondinosaur groups such as the pterosaurs. Dinosaurs are defined as a group that shares certain characteristics. These include: upright limb posture (see opposite), three or fewer phalanges in the fifth finger of the hand, an elongate deltopectoral crest on the humerus, three or more sacral vertebrae, a ball-like head on the femur, and a fully open acetabulum (hip socket in the pelvis).

cervical ribs

dorsal (back) vertebrae

thoracic ribs

scapula (shoulder blade)

coracoid

sacral vertebrae

deltopectoral crest

sternum

humerus

ulna

radius

metacarpals (hand bones)

phalanges (finger bones)

femur (thigh bone)

pelvis

tibia (shin bone)

ischium

fibula

metatarsals (foot bones)

DINOSAUR SKELETON

In most cases, all we know of dinosaurs is their bones and/or teeth. Dinosaurs are tetrapod (four-limbed) vertebrates, as are reptiles, mammals, and birds, so they share the same basic body structure as these other groups. Bones such as the metacarpals (hand bones) are given the same Latin name as those of other vertebrates. The dinosaur shown is *Muttaburrasaurus*, an ornithischian.

UPRIGHT POSTURE

Living lizards and crocodiles have a sprawling gait, with their knees and elbows held out at an angle from their bodies. One of the factors that led to the success of dinosaurs was their upright stance. This provides great advantages over the normal reptilian posture—it allows for longer strides, and therefore faster movement. Early meat-eating archosaurs and dinosaurs were often fast and agile hunters. The upright posture of the dinosaurs also allowed the evolution of bipedal (two-legged) walking.

ENDOTHERMIC?

The traditional view of sluggish, ectothermic (temperature-changing) dinosaurs has largely given way to the theory that most were endothermic (constant temperature). Some were feathered, many were fast runners, and some lived in cold climates that would have been unsuitable for ectothermic animals.

moderately large brain would need endothermic metabolism

close similarities to endothermic birds, including feathers

Velociraptor

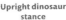

Upright dinosaur stance

Typical sprawling lizard stance

DINOSAUR HIPS

In 1887, the English anatomist Harry Seeley recognized that there were two different types of dinosaur pelvis. Some dinosaurs had a typical lizardlike pelvic structure: Seeley called these saurischian ("lizard-hipped"). Another group had a pelvis that looked like that of modern birds. He called these ornithischian ("bird-hipped"). It is not clear whether the two groups evolved independently or from a common saurischian ancestor.

Saurischian pelvis

The pelvis is made up of the ilium, pubis, and ischium. In most saurischians, the ischium points backward and the pubis points forward.

ilium

acetabulum

ischium   pubis

Ornithischian pelvis

In ornithischian dinosaurs and some rare saurischian groups, the pubis lies against the ischium.

ilium

acetabulum

pubis

ischium

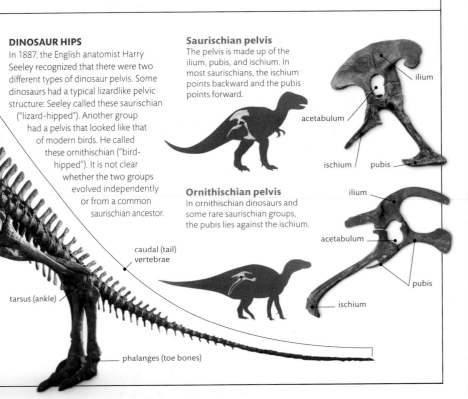

caudal (tail) vertebrae

tarsus (ankle)

phalanges (toe bones)

DINOSAUR AND BIRD EVOLUTION

THE DINOSAURS and their closest relatives were the dominant animals throughout the Mesozoic Era. The first step in the evolution of the dinosaurs occurred in the Permian Period. A new line of reptiles evolved, called the archosaurs ("ruling reptiles"). Some of these developed the ability to walk upright on two feet. The dinosaurs, crocodiles, and the pterosaurs all evolved from these early archosaurs during the Triassic Period. There are two main groups of dinosaurs: the saurischian ("lizard-hipped") group and the ornithischian ("bird-hipped") dinosaurs. Birds evolved from the theropod group of saurischian dinosaurs toward the end of the Jurassic Period. Together with the crocodiles, they are the only surviving archosaurs.

ORNITHISCHIANS

All of the ornithischians were plant-eaters, and they had special adaptations for herbivory. They had a special toothless bone at the tip of the jaw called the predentary, which gave them a toothless beak in front of their teeth. They also had special adaptations to the jaw joint that allowed the teeth to grind against each other (occlude). The first major group to appear were the thyreophorans. This group of armored dinosaurs included the stegosaurs and the ankylosaurs. Another group, the cerapodans, included the ceratopsians, the horned dinosaurs, the pachycephalosaurs, the bone-headed dinosaurs, and the ornithopods, a very diverse group of mainly bipedal dinosaurs.

KEY TO FOSSIL EVIDENCE

 Aves

Paravians

Coelurosaurs

Tetanurans

Sauropodomorphs

Saurischians

Ornithischians

Aves

Paravians

Coelurosaurs

Tetanurans

Ceratosaurs

Sauropodomorphs

Massospondylids

Herrerasaurids

Saurischians

Ankylosaurs

Dinosaurs

Thyreophorans

Ornithischians

Cerapodans

Marginocephalians

PALEOZOIC			MESOZOIC
Carboniferous 359–299mya	Permian 299–252mya	Triassic 252–201mya	Jurassic 201–145mya

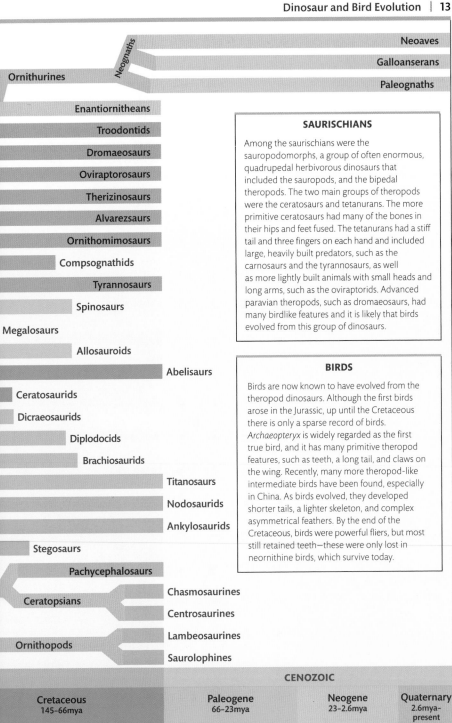

Neoaves

Galloanserans

Neognaths

Ornithurines

Paleognaths

Enantiornitheans

Troodontids

Dromaeosaurs

Oviraptorosaurs

Therizinosaurs

Alvarezsaurs

Ornithomimosaurs

Compsognathids

Tyrannosaurs

Spinosaurs

Megalosaurs

Allosauroids

Abelisaurs

Ceratosaurids

Dicraeosaurids

Diplodocids

Brachiosaurids

Titanosaurs

Nodosaurids

Ankylosaurids

Stegosaurs

Pachycephalosaurs

Ceratopsians

Chasmosaurines

Centrosaurines

Lambeosaurines

Ornithopods

Saurolophines

SAURISCHIANS

Among the saurischians were the sauropodomorphs, a group of often enormous, quadrupedal herbivorous dinosaurs that included the sauropods, and the bipedal theropods. The two main groups of theropods were the ceratosaurs and tetanurans. The more primitive ceratosaurs had many of the bones in their hips and feet fused. The tetanurans had a stiff tail and three fingers on each hand and included large, heavily built predators, such as the carnosaurs and the tyrannosaurs, as well as more lightly built animals with small heads and long arms, such as the oviraptorids. Advanced paravian theropods, such as dromaeosaurs, had many birdlike features and it is likely that birds evolved from this group of dinosaurs.

BIRDS

Birds are now known to have evolved from the theropod dinosaurs. Although the first birds arose in the Jurassic, up until the Cretaceous there is only a sparse record of birds. *Archaeopteryx* is widely regarded as the first true bird, and it has many primitive theropod features, such as teeth, a long tail, and claws on the wing. Recently, many more theropod-like intermediate birds have been found, especially in China. As birds evolved, they developed shorter tails, a lighter skeleton, and complex asymmetrical feathers. By the end of the Cretaceous, birds were powerful fliers, but most still retained teeth—these were only lost in neornithine birds, which survive today.

CENOZOIC			
Cretaceous 145–66mya	Paleogene 66–23mya	Neogene 23–2.6mya	Quaternary 2.6mya–present

MAMMAL EVOLUTION

MAMMALS ARE part of the synapsid lineage of amniotes, which arose during the Carboniferous period. There is debate about which particular groups of mammaliaformes can be considered true mammals, and so there is uncertainty about whether true mammals appeared in the Late Triassic or in the Jurassic. Throughout the Mesozoic, most mammals remained small, but we now know that some lineages diversified in their ecology and some even became large enough to prey on small dinosaurs. After the extinction of the dinosaurs, mammals took over global ecosystems, and today they are represented by three groups: placentals, marsupials, and monotremes.

SYNAPSIDS

The synapsids were a group of amniotes that dominated the land throughout the Permian and much of the Triassic. They had a single opening behind the eye socket on each side of the skull, giving them a more powerful bite. This group also evolved different types of teeth, a feature called heterodonty. These specialized teeth helped them process food in the mouth and improved their digestion. This, in turn, helped more specialized synapsids develop a faster metabolism, using more energy to grow more quickly and be more active. In the Triassic or Jurassic, mammals evolved from one of these specialized synapsid lineages called the cynodonts.

GENETIC EVIDENCE

For more than a century, paleontologists used a classification system of mammals that was based on shared morphological characters, such as the shapes and features of the bones and teeth. This was revolutionized in the early 2000s by studies on the genetic relationships of living mammals using DNA and other molecules. These new techniques showed that many of the groups based on morphology were the result of convergent evolution, where two groups independently evolve the same features because they perform similar functions. Many of the discrepancies in these classification systems have since been solved, and paleontologists now use a combined framework, considering both genetic and morphological data.

KEY TO FOSSIL EVIDENCE

- Placentals
- Marsupials
- Triconodontids
- Mammals
- Mammaliaformes
- Cynodonts
- Dicynodonts
- Sphenacodontid

Mammaliaformes

Cynodonts

Therapsids

Synapsids

Dicynodonts

Sphenacodontids

PALEOZOIC		
Carboniferous 359–299mya	Permian 299–252mya	Triassic 252–201mya

MAMMALIAFORMES

As paleontologists discovered more cynodont fossils, the dividing line between mammals and their ancestors became blurred. Many of the close relatives of mammals had one or more of the defining mammal features, but not all of them. These might include features of the teeth or the specialized mammal-style middle ear. These new fossils now show that many of these features evolved several times independently, rather than in a straightforward way. Paleontologists often call these almost-mammal species "proto-mammals" or lump them together in a paraphyletic group (see p.102) of "mammaliaformes."

Cetaceans

Ruminants

Meridiungulates

Perissodactyls

Cetartiodactyls

Canids

Felids

Carnivorans

Pholidotans

Chiropterans

Eulipotyphlans

Laurasiatherians

Rodents

Lagomorphs

Euarchontoglirans

Primates

Placentals

Xenarthrans

Afrotherians

Mammals

Metatherians

Marsupials

Triconodontids

Multituberculate

Euharamiyids

Monotremes

Docodonts

Morganucodonts

Tritylodontids

MESOZOIC		CENOZOIC		
Jurassic 201–145mya	Cretaceous 145–66mya	Paleogene 66–23mya	Neogene 23–2.6mya	Quaternary 2.6mya–present

GEOLOGICAL TIME

GEOLOGISTS SUBDIVIDE the history of the Earth into very long time intervals called eons. Eons are, in turn, subdivided into eras, eras into periods, and periods into epochs.

The oldest rocks that have survived to be excavated were formed about 4 billion years ago, in the Archean Eon. The earliest fossils come from rocks of about this age.

ROCKS OF AGES

Where rock strata have remained undisturbed, a vertical section through the layers can reveal the rock types laid down during each time period. From these, it is possible to identify the environment (such as desert) and sometimes the age of fossils embedded in that rock, as shown below for rock strata at the Grand Canyon.

ROCK	ENVIRONMENT	PERIOD
Shale, siltstone, mudstone	Tidal flat	Triassic
Limestone	Marine	Permian
Sandstone	Desert	
Shale	Savanna	
Mixed strata—shales, sandstones, limestones	Flood plain	Permian and Late Carboniferous
Limestone	Marine	Early Carboniferous
Limestone	Marine	Devonian
Limestone		Cambrian
Shale	Marine	
Sandstone	Marine	
Complex mixed strata	Marine and volcanic	Precambrian

ERA	TIME	PERIOD
CENOZOIC ERA	2.6 mya–present	QUATERNARY
	23–2.6 mya	NEOGENE
	66–23 mya	PALEOGENE
MESOZOIC ERA	145–66 mya	CRETACEOUS
	201–145 mya	JURASSIC
	252–201 mya	TRIASSIC
PALEOZOIC ERA	299–252 mya	PERMIAN
	359–299 mya	CARBONIFEROUS
	419–359 mya	DEVONIAN
	444–419 mya	SILURIAN
	485–444 mya	ORDOVICIAN
	542–485 mya	CAMBRIAN
	4,600–542 mya	PRECAMBRIAN

4,600 mya	4,000 mya	3,000 mya

Grand Canyon
The Grand Canyon in Arizona provides one of the most impressive displays of sedimentary deposition of rocks. It is over 6,000 ft (2,000 m) deep and shows a clear progression over 300 million years. Layers include sandy limestone, petrified sand dunes, and shale.

Macrauchenia

The ice ages of the Quaternary Period led to the evolution of many mammals adapted to cold climates, such as mammoths. Modern humans evolved.

In the Neogene, large expanses of grassland spread, inhabited by grazing mammals and predatory giant birds. The first hominids evolved from primate ancestors.

Titanis

Ambulocetus

After the end-Cretaceous mass extinctions, mammals evolved into large forms. Some took to a marine way of life. Giant flightless birds evolved.

The Cretaceous was a time of flowering plants, browsing duck-billed dinosaurs, immense tyrannosaurid predators, armored ankylosaurs, and horned ceratopsians.

Didelphodon

Barosaurus

In Jurassic times, the land was dominated by huge sauropods and large predators. A wide variety of pterosaurs evolved. Mammals remained small.

The Triassic marked the dawning of the age of dinosaurs. Advanced synapsids died out after giving rise to mammals.

Herrerasaurus

Synapsids became the dominant land animals during the Permian. The period ended with the largest mass extinction event ever.

Dimetrodon

Tropical forests flourished and oxygen levels were very high during this period. The first reptiles moved onto the land.

Graeophonus

Eastmanosteus

The Devonian Period was a time of rapid evolution. Ammonoids and bony fish evolved and diversified. Trees appeared on land, as did insects and the first four-limbed animals.

Invertebrate species recovered rapidly during the Silurian Period. Primitive lycopods and myriapods became the first true land animals.

Sagenocrinites

Estonioceras

Ordovician seas teemed with primitive fish, trilobites, corals, and shellfish. Plants made their first approaches onto land. The period ended with mass extinctions.

The first animals with skeletons and hard parts such as shells and exoskeletons evolved during the Cambrian "explosion of life." The oceans teemed with trilobites, brachiopods, and the first jawless fish.

Xystridura

Charniodiscus

During the Precambrian, life arose in the oceans—first as single-celled bacteria and algae, then evolving into soft-bodied, multicellular animals, such as jellyfish and worms.

| 2,000 mya | 1,000 mya | 500 mya | 250 mya | 0 |

FOSSIL EVIDENCE

EVIDENCE OF prehistoric life comes from remains (such as bones) that over time have become mineralized to form fossils. Most animal fossils are of creatures that died in or near water. After death, if the hard remains, such as teeth and bones, quickly become covered in mud or sand, dissolved minerals in water are able to seep into the bone pores, initiating a process called permineralization. This reinforces the bones and makes them harder. Sometimes minerals replace the bone completely, petrifying it, or minerals dissolve the bone away, leaving a bone-shaped hollow called a mold.

dinosaur dies near water source

dinosaur's body decomposes in riverbed

river sediments cover skeleton

compressed layers of sand and mud form rock strata

DISCOVERY AND EXCAVATION

Only certain rock types are rich in dinosaur fossils. These include sedimentary sandstones, shales, and mudstones formed in deserts, swamps, and lakes. Most fossil discoveries come from areas where severe erosion exposes deep layers of rock, such as cliffs and mountain slopes, or from places such as quarries and coal mines. Excavating dinosaurs from hard rock may necessitate the use of power tools or explosives. Fossils in desert areas can sometimes be exposed by carefully brushing away the sand covering them.

Excavation
Paleontologists dig around bones to estimate the fossil's state of preservation and size. Delicate scraping and chiseling is needed to reveal delicate structures without causing damage.

skeleton becomes mineralized, enabling it to withstand weight of rock forming overhead

TRACE FOSSILS

Besides fossil remains such as bones, skin impressions, and teeth, dinosaurs left other clues of their existence and lifestyle. Trace fossils include fossil footprint trackways made in mud that dried out in the sun (below right). Coprolites (fossilized droppings) give further clues about a dinosaur's anatomy and lifestyle. Piles of gizzard stones (stones that were swallowed to aid digestion) are also rarely found.

Fossil of the future?

Dinosaur fossils found in the Sahara Desert were formed when the area was a swamp. This camel skeleton may become fossilized if it is buried by the sand.

The fossilization process

Fossilization depends on the rapid covering of remains by sediments that exclude oxygen and thereby arrest the normal processes of decay. In time, minerals from the covering sediments permeate the bone or other tissues, replacing the original material. The soft tissues usually decompose before the process of fossilization begins, so soft-bodied animals, such as jellyfish and worms, are generally poorly preserved.

remains of more recent animals and plants form a separate—"younger"— fossil layer

excavation or natural erosion of rocks reveals fossil-bearing strata

Tracks

Fossilized dinosaur tracks, also called ichnites, can provide information of foot structure, speed, and in what position the tail was held. Importantly, they can also show whether the animal walked on two or four feet. The tracks pictured above are those of a theropod dinosaur.

PRECAMBRIAN TIME
4,600–542 MILLION YEARS AGO

CURRENT ESTIMATES put the age of the Earth at 4,600 million years. The years from that date up until about 542 million years ago (mya) are grouped into one large division of geological time: the Precambrian. This was the time when life first evolved, although evidence of living creatures is sparse. During the first million years of its existence, the world was hot, molten, and totally inhospitable to life. As the earth cooled, volcanic gases and water vapor formed a crude atmosphere and the oceans began to form. Before about 3,000 mya, most of the Earth's surface was volcanic rock, with craters and many unstable regions of volcanic activity. Stable continental areas then began to form. Fossil evidence of life is first seen in rocks dated at 4,200 million years old. The earliest life forms on Earth were simple cells and bacteria. More complex cells and algae first evolved about 1,600 mya. Multicelled plants appeared about 850 mya, whereas the earliest animals (sponges) are about 635–660 million years old.

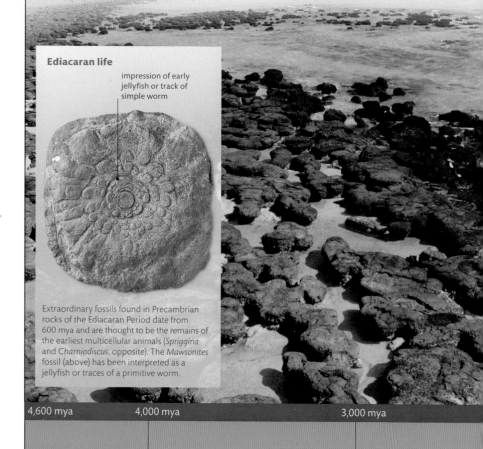

Ediacaran life

impression of early jellyfish or track of simple worm

Extraordinary fossils found in Precambrian rocks of the Ediacaran Period date from 600 mya and are thought to be the remains of the earliest multicellular animals (*Spriggina* and *Charniodiscus*, opposite). The *Mawsonites* fossil (above) has been interpreted as a jellyfish or traces of a primitive worm.

4,600 mya   4,000 mya   3,000 mya

PRECAMBRIAN LANDMASSES

Landmasses began to form about 3,000 mya. About 900 mya, they joined to form the first supercontinent, Rodinia. By 750 mya, Rodinia was sitting across the Equator, but it then started to move southward. This triggered the Cryogenian Period. Between 750 and 650 mya, Rodinia split into two halves (see map), but by the end of the Precambrian, it again formed a single continent called Pannotia.

PRECAMBRIAN LIFE

The first living cells were microscopic organisms possibly living in hot springs. By about 3,500 mya, photosynthesizing algae may have formed layered structures called stromatolites. As oxygen built up in the atmosphere, multicellular animals evolved.

Stromatolites

These layered silica or limestone structures were created by colony-forming algae and provide evidence of early life. *Collenia* (left) was a type of Precambrian stromatolite.

First animals

Late in the Precambrian, the first true animals and plants appeared. *Spriggina* (above) was a strange, long, tapering animal with V-shaped segments running along the length of its body.

Filter feeder

The feather-shaped fossil of *Charniodiscus* is thought to represent an early filter-feeding animal that lived on the sea floor late in the Precambrian.

CAMBRIAN PERIOD

542–485 MILLION YEARS AGO

THE BEGINNING of the Cambrian Period marks the start of the Phanerozoic Era, known as the "Era of Abundant Life." The Cambrian is remarkable for the amazing increase in the number of marine animals and plants. However, the land remained barren. The evolutionary spurt was probably helped by the relatively warm climate. Rapid continental movements led to high sea levels, and large expanses of shallow water covered large parts of the continents. These shallow seas were warm worldwide, as there were no ice caps at either pole.

Burgess Shale
A huge variety of fossil animals, called the Burgess Shale fauna, have been found in shale rocks of the Cambrian Period in British Columbia, Canada. About 180 species of invertebrates have been discovered there. Chordates (creatures with a primitive backbone called a notochord), such as *Pikaia* (right), are also preserved in the Burgess Shale.

notochord
(primitive backbone)

4,600 mya   4,000 mya   3,000 mya

CAMBRIAN LANDMASSES

Continental drift was remarkably rapid during the Cambrian. The supercontinent Pannotia broke up, and the continents moved apart (see map). This caused a rise in sea levels. By 500 mya, the continents of Laurentia, Baltica, and Siberia were lined up along the Equator, with the supercontinent Gondwana (present-day South America, Africa, Antarctica, Australia, and Asia) extending into temperate regions.

CAMBRIAN LIFE
Almost all of the present-day major groupings of animals started to appear during this almost 60-million-year period, including worms, crabs, shellfish, and sponges. Many of the new animals had a hard external skeleton. This provided protection within which multicellular organisms could grow.

Arthropods
This group of early animals were remarkable for being the first organisms with eyes—compound eyes similar to those of insects. *Xystridura* (left), like other arthropods, lived on the seabed and had a skeleton composed of a head shield, a jointed thorax, and a tail shield.

jointed bony thorax with many legs

many small protective plates

Wiwaxia
Many mollusk- and wormlike animals evolved. *Wiwaxia* (right), a mollusklike creature covered in hard spines, lived on the ocean floor.

2,000 mya   1,000 mya   500 mya   250 mya   0

ORDOVICIAN PERIOD

485–444 MILLION YEARS AGO

THE ORDOVICIAN PERIOD saw the first movement of life from the oceans onto the land. Before about 450 mya, the land was barren, apart from mats of algae close to shores. After this time, early forms of liverwort-type plants evolved, possibly from larger algae. They quickly colonized boggy regions and areas around lakes and ponds. In the oceans, the earliest jawless fish (agnathans) appeared, which were mainly tear-drop-shaped animals covered in bony plates. Toward the end of the Ordovician, two extinction events occurred about a million years apart. The first of these was caused by global warming, which resulted in the retreat of glaciers. Warm-water coral reefs died out, and three-quarters of all marine species became extinct within less than a million years.

Brachiopods
Mainly living attached to reefs, these were the most abundant two-shelled organisms in the oceans. *Strophomena* (left) was a medium-sized brachiopod.

4,600 mya	4,000 mya	3,000 mya

ORDOVICIAN LANDMASSES

At the beginning of the Ordovician Period, the supercontinent Gondwana still lay in the southern hemisphere. The other continents were spread out along the Equator and were gradually pushed apart by the expansion of the Iapetus Ocean (see map). Later in the Ordovician Period, the movement of Gondwana toward the South Pole triggered another extinction event. By 440 mya, present-day North Africa lay over the South Pole.

ORDOVICIAN LIFE

The warm equatorial seas that existed for much of the Ordovician were ideal for the evolution of marine life. Coral reefs appeared and soon spread widely. The oceans were also filled with jellyfish, sea anemones, and other colony-forming organisms. A variety of shelled animals, such as brachiopods, lived on the seabed around the reefs.

fanlike colonies held in branching, tubelike structures

segmented body

Graptolites

Graptolites, such as *Rhabdinopora* (above), were unusual colony-forming organisms that floated through the water, feeding through minute tentacles.

Nautiloids

Primitive shelled cephalopods (a group that includes modern cuttlefish) called nautiloids were abundant. Many, such as *Estonioceras* (left), were coiled. They moved by squirting water out of a tube in their body cavity.

Trilobites

The new coral reefs were an ideal habitat for trilobites. *Sphaerexochus* (above) was a typical Ordovician trilobite, with a body of 11 segments.

SILURIAN PERIOD

444–419 MILLION YEARS AGO

BEFORE THE SILURIAN PERIOD, the land had been largely barren apart from some mossy growth and liverworts close to water. The landscape was transformed by the appearance of the first true land plants. These were primitive and simple but had branching stems, roots, and tubes for water transport. Such plants were able to grow to larger sizes than their more primitive predecessors. As areas around water began to be covered by vegetation, soil built up and water became trapped in the land. These conditions allowed the first advances of animal life onto the land. By the end of the Silurian, there were many land arthropods, including primitive centipedes and spider- and scorpionlike arachnids.

SILURIAN LIFE

After the mass extinctions at the end of the Ordovician, evolution progressed at a rapid rate. The earliest true jawed fish appeared, including early members of the cartilaginous fishes (Chondrichthyes) and bony fishes (Osteichthyes). Many new aquatic invertebrates, such as sea urchins, also appeared. Trilobites and mollusks increased in diversity.

12 plated tail segments

small eye

large eye

large, powerful claw

Sea scorpion

The largest Silurian marine invertebrates were the sea scorpions (eurypterids), such as *Pterygotus* (above). In some cases longer than a human, these were the dominant hunters of the early seas, and a few may have been able to crawl ashore. Eurypterids were cousins of horseshoe crabs and arachnids but are not directly related to scorpions.

4,600 mya	4,000 mya	3,000 mya

SILURIAN LANDMASSES

SIBERIA

LAURENTIA BALTICA

GONDWANA

The second Ordovician extinction event led to rising sea levels and flooding of some low-lying areas. The climate became warmer and less seasonal. The supercontinent Gondwana was still lying over the South Pole, with Laurentia sitting astride the Equator (see map). The collision of smaller landmasses formed new mountain ranges. By the end of the Silurian, all of the landmasses were grouped closely together.

freely moving arms

characteristic Y-shaped branching stems

Early plants
The earliest plants, such as *Cooksonia* (left), had a simple branching form. They had water-conducting vessels and reinforced stems.

Crinoids
Despite their plantlike appearance, crinoids (sea lilies) were animals related to starfish and sea urchins. Many species populated Silurian seabeds. *Sagenocrinites* (above) was a small one, with a very compact head and many slender tentacles.

Birkenia
Despite the evolution of the jawed fish, jawless fish (agnathans) were still thriving. *Birkenia* (right) was a freshwater fish that probably fed on the algae that it strained out of muddy lake- and riverbeds.

2,000 mya		1,000 mya	500 mya	250 mya	0

DEVONIAN PERIOD

419–359 MILLION YEARS AGO

DURING THE DEVONIAN, green plants of increasing size started to spread across the landscape. Later in the period, some plants evolved woody tissue, and the first trees appeared. Toward the end of the Devonian, the climate became much warmer. Droughts were common and alternated with periods of heavy rain. Sea levels fell worldwide, and large deserts formed. A wide variety of fish evolved—the Devonian is often called "the Age of Fish." Swampy deltas and river estuaries provided an important habitat for the emergence of animal life onto land.

Prototaxites
Although they looked like tree trunks, *Prototaxites* (right) were actually a type of fungus. Growing up to 26 ft (8 m) tall, they were the largest organisms on land during the Devonian.

Life on land
About 370 mya, the first four-legged vertebrates, such as *Acanthostega* (right), ventured out of the water onto the land. They evolved from one of the groups of lobe-finned fish, whose living relatives are lungfish. The paired fleshy fins of these fish evolved into limbs.

sharp teeth suggest a diet of fish

4,600 mya   4,000 mya   3,000 mya

DEVONIAN LANDMASSES

At the start of the Devonian, the northern landmasses formed one large supercontinent called Laurasia, separated from Gondwana by the Tethys Sea (see map). Huge mountain ranges formed in the future eastern North America and western Europe. By the mid-Devonian, Gondwana and most of Laurasia had moved south of the Equator. The lands that would become China and Siberia were north of the Equator.

DEVONIAN LIFE

The most important evolutionary step during the Devonian was the development of four-limbed land animals. Arthropods also moved onto the land, and the first insects appeared. The oceans teemed with armored jawless fish and the more modern jawed fish. Sharks and ammonoids (a group of mollusks) were common.

Lungfish

Lungfish, such as *Dipterus* (right), have primitive lungs, as well as gills, and survive during seasons of drought by breathing air in watertight burrows in the mud.

pointed fins

body armor

Placoderms

Abundant in Devonian seas, placoderms were jawed fish. Toward the end of the Devonian, some of these creatures reached 26 ft (8 m) in length. *Eastmanosteus* (above), although less than 6½ ft (2 m) long, was a fearsome hunter.

Early sharks

The seas of the Late Devonian teemed with squid, small fish, and crustaceans, which were ideal prey for early sharks such as *Cladoselache* (left). This shark did not have scales on its body.

dorsal fin

| 2,000 mya | | 1,000 mya | 500 mya | 250 mya | 0 |

CARBONIFEROUS PERIOD
359–299 MILLION YEARS AGO

THE CARBONIFEROUS PERIOD opened with tropical conditions over much of the Earth. There were large coastal seas and vast swamps covering the coastal plains. Insects and amphibians found the swamps an ideal environment. Early amphibians looked similar to salamanders, but they soon evolved into many forms, including giant ones. In the warm, moist climate, huge forests of giant tree ferns flourished, producing an oxygen-rich environment. There were also giant horsetails, clubmosses, and seed-bearing plants. Large amounts of decaying vegetation led to the build-up of thick layers of peat, which would later become coal deposits.

CARBONIFEROUS LIFE
There were many types of amphibian tetrapods, ranging from newtlike animals to those the size of crocodiles. By the late Carboniferous, the first reptiles appeared, with the evolution of a shelled egg. The early reptiles were small, but they spread rapidly on land, moving into drier, upland areas.

diamond-shaped leaf bosses

Trees
Huge forests of woody trees, such as *Lepidodendron* (a specimen of fossilized bark is shown left), spread worldwide. This giant clubmoss had a columnlike trunk with skeletal, spreading branches and could grow to heights of 115 ft (35 m), with a trunk diameter of over 6½ ft (2 m).

small, slim, yet sturdy body

First reptile?
When first discovered, *Westlothiana lizziae* (right) was hailed as the first real reptile. It is now regarded as reptilelike rather than a true reptile. *Westlothiana* has features that indicate an evolutionary position between primitive tetrapods and true reptiles.

Insects and arthropods
Already populous by the Carboniferous, insects and arthropods continued to diversify. *Graephonus* (above) was a whip scorpion, with six legs and a pair of pincers.

4,600 mya	4,000 mya		3,000 mya

CARBONIFEROUS LANDMASSES

At the beginning of the Carboniferous, most of the Earth's landmasses were arranged in two great supercontinents: Laurasia in the north and Gondwana in the south (see map). Later in the Carboniferous, they moved closer together. Gondwana started to move over the South Pole again. The advance and retreat of the ensuing ice sheets led to at least two ice ages in the last half of the Carboniferous.

Life in a swamp

The spread of the forests raised oxygen levels around the world, and this factor, combined with the increasingly humid conditions, may have allowed the evolution of very large amphibians and insects. Crocodilelike amphibians, such as *Eryops*, hunted at the bottom of the swamps. The largest Carboniferous dragonflies had wingspans of up to 2½ ft (75 cm), and some early scorpions were more than 2 ft (60 cm) long.

early reptiles, such as **Hylonomus**, migrated to drier areas

the dragonfly **Meganeura**, one of the largest flying insects

Eryops, a large, amphibian aquatic hunter

PERMIAN PERIOD

299–252 MILLION YEARS AGO

THE PERMIAN was a time of dramatic climatic changes. At the start of the Permian, Gondwana was still in the grip of an ice age. It gradually warmed over the next few million years as it moved northward. Large parts of Laurasia became very hot and dry, and massive expanses of desert formed. This had a damaging effect on amphibian populations: they were confined to the fewer damp areas, and many species became extinct. This provided the opportunity for reptiles to spread more widely and diversify. Continental upheavals and further extreme climate changes at the end of the Permian led to the largest mass extinction event ever. More than half of all animal families became extinct.

PERMIAN LIFE

Reptiles continued to spread rapidly. Among the dominant land animals of the time were the synapsids (mammal-like reptiles). By the mid Permian, these had diversified into the therapsids. Later in the period, a mammal-like group of therapsids called the cynodonts ("dog teeth") evolved.

bony spike

Pareiasaurs

These were large, primitive, herbivorous reptiles. *Elginia* (a fossil skull is shown left) was one of the smaller pareiasaurs and one of the last of the group.

broad vertebrae at base of spine

Early parareptile

Procolophon (right) was a member of the Parareptilia—a clade of reptiles. It may have eaten insects. Later members of its family were larger and had teeth designed for eating plants.

ribs enclosing rounded body

PERMIAN LANDMASSES

Throughout the Permian Period, Laurasia in the north and Gondwana in the south continued to move closer together (see map). By the end of the period, they collided to form the giant supercontinent of Pangea. This straddled the Equator and was bounded to the east by the shallow Tethys Sea. Many shallow coastal seas disappeared, inland desert areas became much larger, and sea levels fell worldwide.

Synapsids

One of the best-known of this group of early Permian predators, *Dimetrodon* (left) had a distinctive sail on its back, which was supported by bony rods. This is thought to have been for heat exchange or sexual display.

large, sharp teeth indicate carnivorous lifestyle

2,000 mya · 1,000 mya · · · · · 500 mya · · · 250 mya · · 0

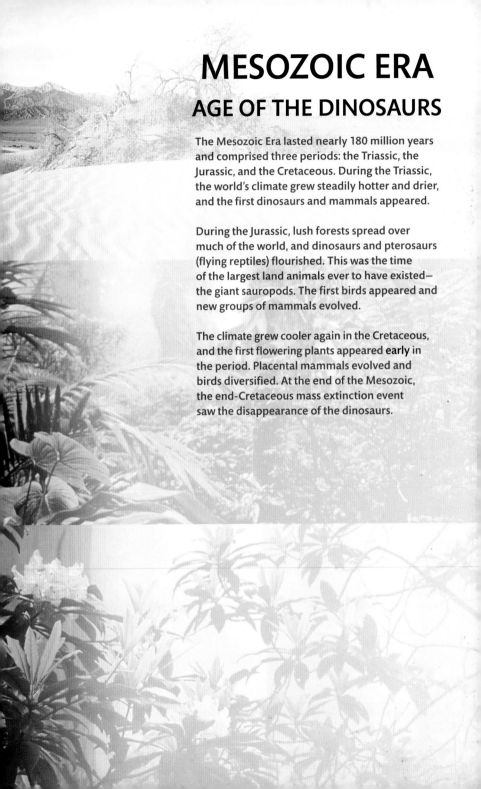

MESOZOIC ERA

AGE OF THE DINOSAURS

The Mesozoic Era lasted nearly 180 million years and comprised three periods: the Triassic, the Jurassic, and the Cretaceous. During the Triassic, the world's climate grew steadily hotter and drier, and the first dinosaurs and mammals appeared.

During the Jurassic, lush forests spread over much of the world, and dinosaurs and pterosaurs (flying reptiles) flourished. This was the time of the largest land animals ever to have existed—the giant sauropods. The first birds appeared and new groups of mammals evolved.

The climate grew cooler again in the Cretaceous, and the first flowering plants appeared **early** in the period. Placental mammals evolved and birds diversified. At the end of the Mesozoic, the end-Cretaceous mass extinction event saw the disappearance of the dinosaurs.

TRIASSIC PERIOD
252–201 MILLION YEARS AGO

AFTER THE MASS extinctions at the end of the Permian, the oceans and land were left startlingly empty of life. It took about 10 million years for the Earth's ecosystems to recover. During the Triassic, the surviving reptile groups spread widely and the first true dinosaurs appeared. A large area of the world's landmasses lay in the equatorial belt, and interior regions were subject to alternating seasons of heavy monsoonal rains and drought. The climate was generally warm, and there were no polar ice caps. These conditions favored certain types of plants, such as seed ferns and conifers, which could cope with arid conditions, and horsetails in damper areas. The climate grew even drier at the end of the Triassic.

TRIASSIC LIFE

Most of the synapsids, which had dominated the land in Permian times, did not survive into the Triassic. The surviving groups radiated again but lost a number of their ecological niches to new reptile groups—the archosaurs ("ruling reptiles") and the rhynchosaurs (a short-lived group of diapsid reptiles). Several lines of aquatic reptiles also evolved. These were the nothosaurs, placodonts, and ichthyosaurs. The Late Triassic saw the arrival of the dinosaurs, crocodilians, pterosaurs, turtles, and primitive mammals.

saurischian ("lizard-hipped") pelvic structure

Cynodonts

The cynodonts (doglike mammal ancestors) were a group that survived into the Triassic. *Cynognathus* (above) was a large Triassic carnivorous cynodont.

First dinosaurs

The earliest dinosaurs evolved about 230 mya. *Herrerasaurus* (right) and *Eoraptor*, both found in Argentina, are thought to be among the earliest dinosaurs. Both of them were agile bipedal hunters.

long toe bones

4,600 mya	4,000 mya	3,000 mya

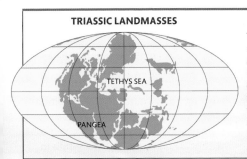

TRIASSIC LANDMASSES

TETHYS SEA

PANGEA

The supercontinent Pangea reached its maximum state of fusion in the mid Triassic about 230 mya. Parts of present-day Asia may have formed islands, but most of the landmasses of the Earth were in contact. Pangea straddled the Equator, reaching from pole to pole. The temperature gradient between the Equator and the poles was far less extreme than it is in modern times, and there were no polar ice caps.

Flying reptiles

The earliest known flying reptiles are pterosaurs, found in Late Triassic deposits. They were accomplished flyers with wings made of skin attached to an elongated fourth finger. *Peteinosaurus* (above) was an early pterosaur (a primitive form) with a short neck and a long, bony tail.

Triassic vegetation

Many plants of the Paleozoic Era relied on high rainfall and damp conditions. *Dicroidium* (right) was a seed fern the size of a small tree. It thrived in swampy areas of the Triassic southern hemisphere. In many areas, however, such tropical vegetation was gradually replaced by plants, such as cycads, ginkgos, and evergreen trees, which were better suited to the prevailing arid conditions.

opposing pairs of leaflets

"Y"-forked leaf

2,000 mya   1,000 mya   500 mya   250 mya   0

DIAPSIDS

AFTER THE end-Permian extinction, surviving diapsids slowly recovered and began to occupy some of the ecological roles previously filled by synapsids.

Most major diapsid groups had originated prior to the extinction, but in the Triassic they underwent significant radiations. Early in the Triassic, some diapsids returned to the sea, leading to the ichthyosaur and sauropterygian lineages, but the origins of these groups are still a mystery. Placodonts were among the successful colonizers of the oceans, but they would not survive the Triassic–Jurassic extinction. They developed turtlelike shells to protect them from the carnivorous sauropterygians, but they were only distantly related to turtles.

Lepidosaurs diversified, too, and early in the Triassic the first squamates (the group to which lizards and snakes belong) appeared. The most successful Triassic diapsids were the archosauromorphs, including pseudosuchians and dinosaurs, alongside some groups with no modern descendants, such as pterosaurs, phytosaurs, and rhynchosaurs.

Pterosaurs, the first vertebrates to evolve powered flight, took to the skies early in the Triassic. Pseudosuchians, the broad group that gave rise to modern crocodiles, were the dominant terrestrial animals for most of the Triassic, and they developed a staggering diversity that included top carnivores, lumbering herbivores, and agile bipeds. For reasons still unclear, however, they were slowly displaced by dinosaurs toward the end of the Triassic. The first dinosaurs were small carnivores, but by the end of the Triassic there were also large herbivorous sauropodomorphs, such as *Plateosaurus*.

Group: SAUROPTERYGIA	Subgroup: Placodontia	Time: 237–227 mya

Henodus

HEN-OH-DUS

shell formed of irregular bony plates and horn

Henodus ("single-tooth") was an armored placodont shaped like a modern turtle. It was as wide as it was long, and its back and belly were protected by bony, many-sided plates that made up a defensive shell. This in turn was completely covered with plates of tough horn. *Henodus* lived in near-shore marine environments. It had a strangely square snout and one tooth per side of the mouth. It also had a horny beak at the front of the mouth, similar to that of modern turtles. *Henodus* scraped plants off the bottom using suction and filter feeding. Its short, clawed feet may have been webbed.

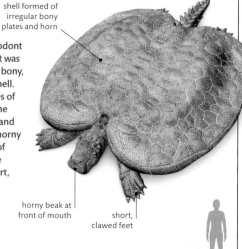

horny beak at front of mouth

short, clawed feet

DESCRIBED BY
Huene 1936
HABITAT
Lagoons

Length: 3¼ ft (1 m)	Weight: Not calculated	Diet: Herbivore or filter feeder

Group: SAUROPTERYGIA	Subgroup: Placodontia	Time: 243–235 mya

Placodus

PLAK-OH-DUS

This placodont shows few adaptations for an aquatic lifestyle, with a stocky body, short neck, and sprawling limbs. However, there were webs of skin between the toes, and the tail was flattened from side to side. There may also have been a fin on the tail. *Placodus* ("flat tooth") had forward-pointing teeth used to pluck shellfish off rocks. Flat teeth on the palate met other teeth on the lower jaw to produce an efficient crushing action.

DESCRIBED BY Agassiz 1843
HABITAT Seashores

flat teeth

Lower jaw   Upper jaw

sprawling, five-toed feet

belly ribs formed protective shell

Length: 6½ ft (2 m)	Weight: Not calculated	Diet: Shellfish, crustaceans

Group: SAUROPTERYGIA	Subgroup: Placodontia	Time: 227–201 mya

Psephoderma

SEF-OH-DER-MAH

This relatively well-known placodont was remarkably turtlelike in appearance. Its body was broad and flat and covered with hexagonal plates. Its limbs were paddle-shaped. *Psephoderma* ("pebble skin") had great biting power—a horny beak at the front of its mouth could pluck shellfish, which were then crushed by its teeth and jaws.

DESCRIBED BY von Meyer 1858
HABITAT Shallow seas

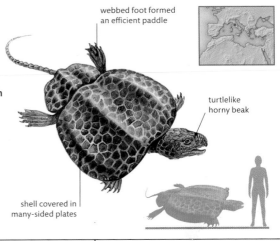

webbed foot formed an efficient paddle

turtlelike horny beak

shell covered in many-sided plates

Length: 6 ft (1.8 m)	Weight: Not calculated	Diet: Shellfish, crustaceans

Group: SAUROPTERYGIA	Subgroup: Nothosauria	Time: 242 mya

Ceresiosaurus

SER-EE-SEE-OH-SAW-RUS

Ceresiosaurus ("lizard of Lugano") had toes that were much longer than those of other nothosaurs due to hyperphalangy (an increased number of bones in each toe). The length of its feet, which may have been webbed, meant that efficient swimming flippers were formed. The forelegs were longer than the hind legs, suggesting that they were the ones used most for steering. *Ceresiosaurus* swam using a combination of its large front flippers for propulsion and undulation of the body.

DESCRIBED BY Peyer 1931
HABITAT Shallow seas

flattened, high tail

long, flexible neck

streamlined body

nostrils very high on head

longer front legs than hind

Length: 10 ft (3 m)	Weight: ~200 lb (90 kg)	Diet: Fish

Group: SAUROPTERYGIA	Subgroup: Nothosauria	Time: 247–237 mya

Lariosaurus

LA-REE-OH-SAW-RUS

Lariosaurus was a small member of the nothosaur group of marine reptiles. It had primitive adaptations to an aquatic lifestyle. Its neck and toes were very short, and the webs of skin on its hind feet would have been small and therefore not much use for fast swimming. Its front feet formed paddlelike flippers. In common with other members of its group, it had flexible knee and ankle joints. Fossil embryos preserved with an adult *Lariosaurus* show that it gave birth to live young, an adaptation that would have allowed it to reproduce without returning to land.

DESCRIBED BY
Curioni 1847
HABITAT
Coastal shallows

Length: 24 in (60 cm)	Weight: ~22 lb (10 kg)	Diet: Small fish, shrimp

Group: SAUROPTERYGIA	Subgroup: Nothosauria	Time: 240–210 mya

Nothosaurus

NOH-THO-SAW-RUS

Nothosaurus ("false lizard") was a typical nothosaur. Its long body, neck, and tail were flexible and moderately streamlined. Some fossils have impressions of webbed skin between the five toes of the feet. The head was slim and the jaws contained many sharp, thin teeth that interlocked when the mouth was closed. The nostrils were placed high on the head, close to the eyes.

DESCRIBED BY
Munster 1834
HABITAT
Coastal regions

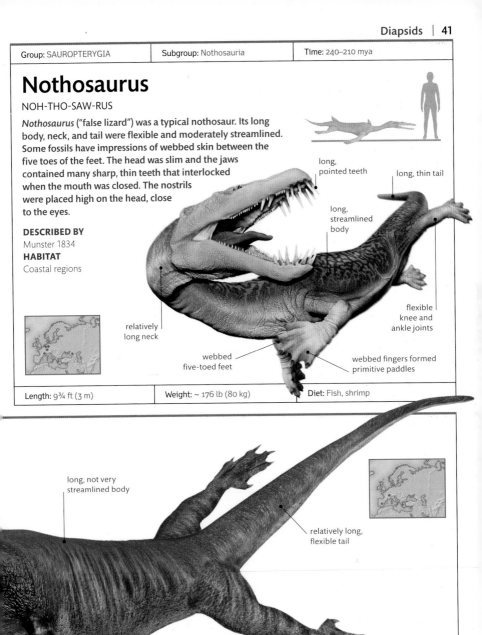

long, pointed teeth

long, thin tail

long, streamlined body

flexible knee and ankle joints

relatively long neck

webbed five-toed feet

webbed fingers formed primitive paddles

long, not very streamlined body

relatively long, flexible tail

primitive paddlelike flipper

five slightly webbed toes with claws

Length: 9¾ ft (3 m)	Weight: ~ 176 lb (80 kg)	Diet: Fish, shrimp

Group: ICHTHYOPTERYGIA	Subgroup: Ichthyosauria	Time: 247–242 mya

Mixosaurus

MIX-OH-SAW-RUS

This "mixed reptile" is thought to have been an intermediate form between primitive ichthyosaurs and more advanced types. It had a fishlike body, typical of advanced ichthyosaurs, with a dorsal fin on its back. However, it only had a small fin on the top of its tail. Its paddles were short, with the front pair longer than the hind ones.

DESCRIBED BY Baur 1887
HABITAT Oceans

rudimentary
tail fin

small dorsal fin

short hind
flippers

long, narrow
jaws with
sharp teeth

Length: 3¼ ft (1 m)	Weight: Not calculated	Diet: Fish

Group: ICHTHYOPTERYGIA	Subgroup: Ichthyosauria	Time: 237–210 mya

Shonisaurus

SHON-EE-SAW-RUS

Shonisaurus ("Shoshone mountain reptile") is the largest ichthyosaur known. It had the typical ichthyosaur shape, with its head and neck, body, and tail making up equal thirds of its length. However, it had several features that indicate that it was an offshoot from the main ichthyosaur line. Its jaws were very long and had teeth only at the front. Its paddles were also unusually long and of equal length.

DESCRIBED BY Camp 1976
HABITAT Oceans

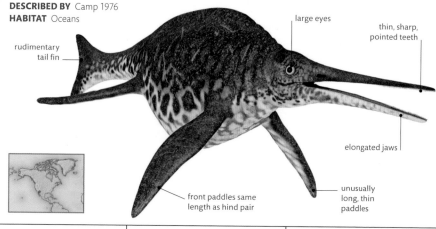

rudimentary
tail fin

large eyes

thin, sharp,
pointed teeth

elongated jaws

front paddles same
length as hind pair

unusually
long, thin
paddles

Length: 69 ft (21 m)	Weight: ~20–35 tons (20.3–35.5 metric tons)	Diet: Fish, squid, other cephalopods

Group: DIAPSIDA	Subgroup: Tanystropheidae	Time: 230 mya

Tanystropheus

TAN-EE-STRO-FEE-US

This reptile is one of the strangest to have ever existed. Its incredibly long neck was composed of only 13 vertebrae, which were so elongated that they were first thought to be leg bones. The neck length has led to much speculation about this animal's lifestyle, as it was not well-adapted for either walking or swimming. Current opinion is that it used its neck to fish from sea or lake shores or from shallow water.

DESCRIBED BY von Meyer 1852
HABITAT Shorelines

neck made up half animal's length

slender forelimbs with small hands

long feet may have been webbed

Fishing grounds
The neck of *Tanystropheus* was so long that it may have been able to fish while lying on lake or sea shores.

Length: 20 ft (6 m)	Weight: ~330 lb (150 kg)	Diet: Fish

Group: ARCHOSAUROMORPHA	Subgroup: Rhynchosauria	Time: 230–227 mya

Hyperodapedon

HI-PER-OH-DA-PEE-DON

This rhynchosaur was abundant in the Mid Triassic. It had a squat, short, barrel-shaped body, with a large head and moderately long tail. Its mouth ended in a beak, used to nip off vegetation, and its teeth were designed for efficient chopping of tough plant material. It had several rows of teeth on the upper jaw. A groove ran through the middle row of teeth; and, on the lower jaw, a single row of teeth fitted into it when the mouth was closed.

DESCRIBED BY
Huxley 1859
HABITAT
Woodland

short, stout legs

large body cavity

relatively long tail

small beak at front of snout

Length: 4 ft (1.2 m)	Weight: ~88 lb (40 kg)	Diet: Seed ferns

Group: ARCHOSAUROMORPHA	Subgroup: Archosauriformes	Time: 252–247 mya

Proterosuchus

PRO-TEH-RO-SU-KUSS

Proterosuchus was one of the earliest known archosaurs. It had a large, heavy body, and its legs were angled out from the body, resulting in a sprawling, lizardlike gait. It probably lived a lifestyle similar to that of crocodiles, spending most of its time hunting in rivers. Its teeth were sharp and curved backward, and there were also primitive teeth on the palate. *Proterosuchus* had a pointed, downwardly hooked snout.

DESCRIBED BY Broom 1903
HABITAT Riverbanks

long, heavy tail

large head with long snout

sprawling, stout limbs

Length: 6½ ft (2 m)	Weight: Not calculated	Diet: Fish, herbivorous dicynodonts

Group: ARCHOSAURIFORMES	Subgroup: Pseudosuchia	Time: 222–212 mya

Parasuchus

PAR-A-SOOK-US

Parasuchus, whose name means "near crocodile," looked remarkably like a modern crocodile. Its throat and back were protected by heavy armored plates (or scutes) and the belly was strengthened by a dense arrangement of abdominal ribs. The skull was long, with a slender snout. The jaws were lined with conical teeth. Nostrils positioned on top of the head allowed *Parasuchus* to breathe while underwater.

DESCRIBED BY Lydekker 1885
HABITAT Riverbanks and marshy areas

back protected by heavy scutes

nostrils on top of snout

Length: 8¼ ft (2.5 m)	Weight: Not calculated	Diet: Fish

Group: ARCHOSAURIFORMES	Subgroup: Pseudosuchia	Time: 235–206 mya

Stagonolepis

STAG-ON-OH-LEP-IS

Like other members of its family, *Stagonolepis* was herbivorous and had a deep, low-slung body adapted to accommodate the longer intestines needed for digesting plants. It was heavily armored, with rectangular plates covering the whole of the back and tail. A row of short spikes ran along each side of the animal, and the underside of the belly and tail was covered with more bony plates.

DESCRIBED BY
Agassiz 1844
HABITAT Forests

rectangular plates of bony armor

five-toed feet

peglike teeth at back of jaw

Length: 2.5m (8¼ft)	Weight: ~200kg (440lb)	Diet: Plants

Group: ARCHOSAURIFORMES	Subgroup: Pseudosuchia	Time: 228–200 mya

Desmatosuchus

DES-MAT-OH-SOOK-US

Desmatosuchus ("link crocodile") was a particularly heavily armored animal that superficially resembled a short-snouted crocodile. Rows of rectangular plates covered its back and tail, and a row of short spikes ran along the flanks. Long spikes jutted out from each shoulder. The underside of the belly was also covered in bony plates. The body was long and deep, with relatively short legs. The cheek teeth were weak and peglike.

DESCRIBED BY Case 1920
HABITAT Forests

toothless snout

rectangular bony plates along back and tail

shoulder spikes up to 18 in (45 cm) long

Length: 16 ft (5 m)	Weight: ~660 lb (300 kg)	Diet: Plants

Group: ARCHOSAUROMORPHA	Subgroup: Archosauriformes	Time: 235 mya

Euparkeria

EWE-PARK-ER-EE-A

Euparkeria was an early archosaur and was unusual among its contemporaries in that the relative length of its hind legs to its forelegs was greater than that of contemporary reptiles. It probably spent most of its time on all fours but was capable of rising onto its hind legs to run. Its tail made up about half its body weight and was held outstretched for balance as it ran. The body was small and slim, with thin, bony plates covering the middle of the back and tail. The head was large but light, and the many teeth were sharp, serrated, and curved backward, indicating a carnivorous way of life.

ridge of light bony plates running along back

DESCRIBED BY
Broom 1913
HABITAT Woodland

lightly built head despite large size

four-fingered hands

Length: 24 in (60 cm)	Weight: ~30 lb (13.5 kg)	Diet: Meat

Group: ARCHOSAURIA	Subgroup: Pterosauria	Time: 227–208 mya

Peteinosaurus

PET-INE-OH-SAW-RUS

Peteinosaurus ("winged lizard") is one of the earliest vertebrates to show evidence of active, flapping flight. It had a light-boned skeleton, like that of a modern bird. Its long tail was stiffened with bony ligaments to stabilize it during flight. It had cone-shaped teeth for crunching insects.

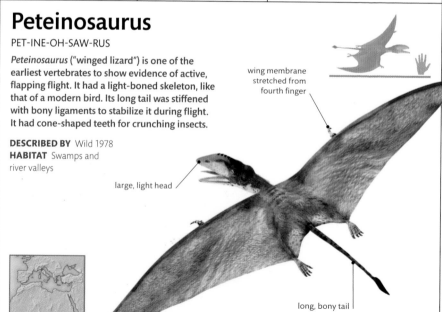

wing membrane stretched from fourth finger

DESCRIBED BY Wild 1978
HABITAT Swamps and river valleys

large, light head

long, bony tail

Length: 24 in (60 cm)	Weight: Not calculated	Diet: Flying insects

Group: ARCHOSAURIA	Subgroup: Pterosauria	Time: 217–208 mya

Eudimorphodon

U-DI-MORF-OH-DON

This pterosaur was typical of its group, with a short neck; large head; and long, bony tail stiffened by a network of bony ligaments. It had a diamond-shaped flap at the tail tip, which probably acted as a rudder. Its breastbone structure shows that it was capable of flapping its wings.

DESCRIBED BY Zambelli 1973
HABITAT Shores

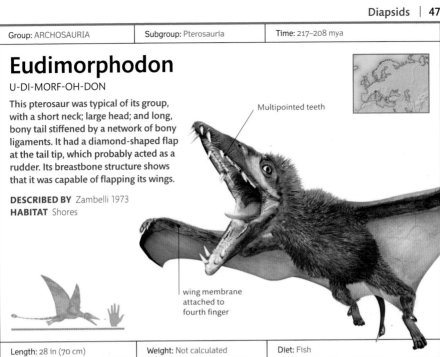

Multipointed teeth

wing membrane attached to fourth finger

Length: 28 in (70 cm)	Weight: Not calculated	Diet: Fish

Group: ARCHOSAURIA	Subgroup: Dinosauromorpha	Time: 230 mya

Lagosuchus

LAY-GO-SOOK-US

Lagosuchus, or "rabbit crocodile," belonged to the group that gave rise to the dinosaurs, although it is unlikely that it was their direct ancestor. It was indeed strikingly similar in appearance to small, early theropod dinosaurs. Its body was slim and lightly built; the tail was long and flexible; and the hind legs were long and thin, with shin bones much longer than the thighs. *Lagosuchus* ran on its hind legs.

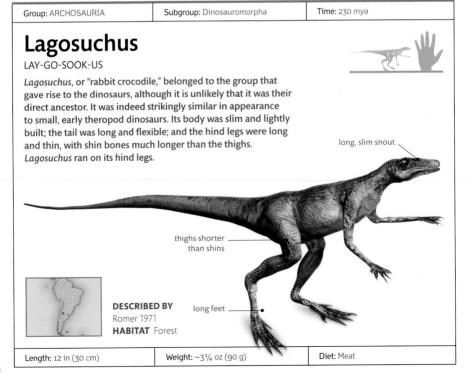

long, slim snout

thighs shorter than shins

DESCRIBED BY
Romer 1971
HABITAT Forest

long feet

Length: 12 in (30 cm)	Weight: ~3¼ oz (90 g)	Diet: Meat

Group: SAURISCHIA	Subgroup: Herrerasauridae	Time: 233 mya

Gnathovorax

NATH-OH-VOR-ACKS

Gnathovorax ("devouring jaw") is known from the most complete skeleton of any herrerasaurid. An analysis of its teeth shows that it was a carnivore, and its diet may have consisted of rhynchosaurs and cynodonts, which were found with the skeleton in Brazil. Its brain was still primitive, but the regions that controlled the eyes and head were enlarged, probably for its predatory lifestyle.

DESCRIBED BY Pacheco et al. 2019
HABITAT Semiarid coastal plains

primitive brain

sharp teeth for carnivorous diet

four-fingered, grasping hands

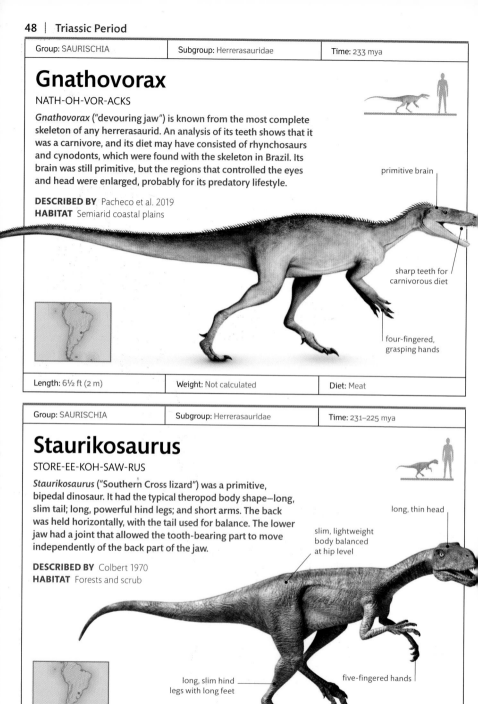

Length: 6½ ft (2 m)	Weight: Not calculated	Diet: Meat

Group: SAURISCHIA	Subgroup: Herrerasauridae	Time: 231–225 mya

Staurikosaurus

STORE-EE-KOH-SAW-RUS

Staurikosaurus ("Southern Cross lizard") was a primitive, bipedal dinosaur. It had the typical theropod body shape—long, slim tail; long, powerful hind legs; and short arms. The back was held horizontally, with the tail used for balance. The lower jaw had a joint that allowed the tooth-bearing part to move independently of the back part of the jaw.

DESCRIBED BY Colbert 1970
HABITAT Forests and scrub

long, thin head

slim, lightweight body balanced at hip level

five-fingered hands

long, slim hind legs with long feet

Length: 6½ ft (2 m)	Weight: ~44–88 lb (20–40 kg)	Diet: Meat

Group: SAURISCHIA	Subgroup: Herrerasauridae	Time: 228 mya

Herrerasaurus

HERR-RAY-RAH-SAW-RUS

Analysis of a complete skeleton of *Herrerasaurus* ("Herrera's lizard") discovered in the 1990s confirmed that it was one of the most primitive dinosaurs. However, paleontologists are still disputing whether it can be classified as a theropod. *Herrerasaurus* was an agile hunter, probably able to prey on slower creatures such as *Hyperodapedon* (see p.43). It had powerful hindlimbs and a long tail used for balance. It probably ran with its back nearly horizontal to balance the body at the hips. The jaws were lined with sharp, long teeth that were curved backward. New evidence suggests that the skull was more boxy than tapered at the snout.

DESCRIBED BY Reig 1963
HABITAT Woodland

small ridge running down snout

long, sharp teeth

probably scaly skin

tail held outstretched for balance

sturdy thighs

claws on three fingers

skull lightened by holes

four-toed feet

long, flexible tail

strong, grasping arms and hands

ridge running down front edge of humerus

Skeletal reconstruction

Length: 10 ft (3.1 m)	Weight: ~460 lb (210 kg)	Diet: Meat

Group: SAURISCHIA	Subgroup: Sauropodomorpha	Time: 210 mya

Efraasia

EE-FRAA-ZIA

This early sauropodomorph was named after its discoverer, E. Fraas. It was lightly built, with a small head, fairly long neck, and long tail. Its legs were longer than its arms, and its five-fingered hands had a large thumb claw. It may have walked on all fours to browse and risen onto its hind legs to run.

DESCRIBED BY Galton 1973
HABITAT Dry upland plains

nostrils far
forward
on snout

flexible tail

five long digits
on hands

Length: 21 ft (6.5 m)	Weight: ~880 lb (400 kg)	Diet: Plants, possibly some meat

Group: SAURISCHIA	Subgroup: Sauropodomorpha	Time: 203–201 mya

Thecodontosaurus

THEE-COH-DONT-OH-SAW-RUS

This dinosaur was one of the earliest dinosaurs to be discovered, but it was not recognized as a dinosaur until later. *Thecodontosaurus* is one of the most primitive sauropodomorphs known. Its name ("socket-toothed lizard") was given because its saw-edged teeth were embedded in the sockets in the jaw bones. *Thecodontosaurus* had a relatively small head and a long tail. Mainly bipedal, it seems to have had some ability to walk on all fours.

fairly
short neck

small head

DESCRIBED BY Riley and Stutchbury 1836
HABITAT
Desert plains, dry upland areas

four-toed feet

large
thumb claw

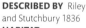

Length: 7 ft (2.1 m)	Weight: ~110 lb (50 kg)	Diet: Plants, possibly omnivorous

Group: SAURISCHIA	Subgroup: Sauropodomorpha	Time: 214–204 mya

Plateosaurus

PLAT-EE-OH-SAW-RUS

This "broad lizard" was one of the most common
dinosaurs of the Late Triassic Period. The large number
of fossil finds suggest that *Plateosaurus* may have lived
in herds and migrated to avoid seasonal droughts. It
walked on its hind legs and gathered food from high
vegetation. The thumbs on its hands were partially
opposable, allowing it to grasp food. Its small skull
was deeper than in most other sauropodomorphs
and its fairly short neck was thinner. *Plateosaurus* had
many small, leaf-shaped teeth, and the hinge of the
lower jaw was low-slung to give greater leverage. These
factors indicate a diet primarily composed of plants.
This dinosaur also had a very large nasal chamber,
but the reason for this is as yet unknown.

DESCRIBED BY Meyer 1837
HABITAT Dry plains, desert

beaklike
upper jaw

fairly short, thin,
flexible neck

bulky
body

low hinge
on lower jaw

long finger
and hand
bones

strong
thigh bone

flexible tail
about half
dinosaur's
length

Skeletal reconstruction

clawed
fingers

hindlimbs
longer than
forelimbs

three forward-facing
clawed toes

Length: 26 ft (8 m)	Weight: ~4.4 tons (4 metric tons)	Diet: Leaves, small amounts of meat

Group: SAURISCHIA	Subgroup: Sauropodomorpha	Time: 228 mya

Eoraptor

EE-OH-RAP-TOR

Eoraptor ("dawn raptor") is regarded as one of the earliest dinosaurs. It was a very small, lightly built, bipedal carnivore with hollow bones. The head was long and slim, with many small, sharp teeth. The arms were far shorter than the legs and had five-fingered hands, although two of the fingers were reduced. *Eoraptor* appears to lack the specialized features of any of the major groups of dinosaurs and for this reason is consistent with what would be expected for the earliest dinosaur ancestors.

DESCRIBED BY Sereno et al. 1993
HABITAT Forests

small, sharp teeth

five-fingered hands

Length: 39 in (1 m)	Weight: ~22 lbs (10 kg)	Diet: Meat

Group: SAURISCHIA	Subgroup: Theropoda	Time: 213–190 mya

Coelophysis

SEE-LOW-FIE-SIS

Coelophysis ("hollow face") was a small, lightly built, early dinosaur with open skull bones (hence its name). The body was long and slim and the head was pointed, with many small, serrated teeth. *Coelophysis* is one of the best-known dinosaurs due to the excavation of dozens of skeletons from New Mexico (see right). Many of these fossils contained the remains of their prey. It was suggested that these were bones of young *Coelophysis* and it was seen as evidence of cannibalism. However, the bones are now interpreted to be those of some kind of crocodylomorph.

small, pointed teeth

hands with three fingers and a fourth rudimentary digit

DESCRIBED BY
Cope 1889
HABITAT
Desert plains

Length: 10 ft (3.1 m)	Weight: ~44 lb (22 kg)	Diet: Meat, perhaps including birds, carrion

long tail

long, slim legs

four-toed feet

long, flexible tail

Ghost Ranch, New Mexico
Many fossil skeletons of *Coelophysis* have been found at this site.

long hind legs

remains of prey in abdominal cavity

three long, forward-facing, clawed toes

Fossil skeleton embedded in rock

SYNAPSIDS

SYNAPSIDS WERE HIT particularly hard in the end-Permian extinction. Therapsids, which had replaced pelycosaurs as the dominant synapsids in the Permian, were represented only by a few survivors. These were mostly small, rapidly breeding burrowers that were able to quickly adapt to the harsh Early Triassic landscape.

Gorgonopsians, the Permian top predators, went extinct in the end-Permian extinction. Dicynodonts survived, and in the Early Triassic they were incredibly abundant throughout the world. Alongside the diapsid rhynchosaurs, dicynodonts became important large herbivores, with some, such as *Lisowicia*, reaching the size of elephants. Despite their success, they went extinct at the end of the Triassic.

Another surviving therapsid lineage, the cynodonts, eventually occupied a wide range of ecological niches—including large carnivores and herbivores—but it was the smaller members of this group that would be the most successful. These nocturnal insectivores became highly specialized, developing complex teeth, keen hearing, and coats of fur for insulation. These changes were linked to a shift in metabolism, and these small cynodonts started to produce and regulate their own body heat. This new lifestyle required huge amounts of energy to sustain, but it helped them stay active regardless of environmental conditions. Cynodonts were the only synapsid survivors of the Triassic, and their descendants, the mammals, still thrive today.

Group: THERAPSIDA	Subgroup: Dicynodontia	Time: 247–242 mya

Sinokannemeyeria

SY-NOH-KAN-EH-MEY-REE-A

This long-snouted member of the dicynodont ("two-dog teeth") group of synapsids was well adapted for a lifestyle as a terrestrial herbivore. Its head was massive, with large openings for the eyes, nostrils, and jaw muscles. These reduced the weight of the skull. A hinge between the lower jaw and the skull allowed the jaws to move backward and forward with a shearing action. Although the jaws were toothless, this motion would have ground up the toughest vegetation. The front of the jaw had a small horn-covered beak, and there were two small tusks growing from bulbous projections on the upper jaw. These tusks could have been used to dig up roots. *Sinokannemeyeria* had relatively short, stumpy legs, which were held in a slightly sprawling gait to the sides of its body. The limb girdles were formed into large, heavy plates of bone to support the weight of the wide, heavily built body. *Sinokannemeyeria* was probably not a fast or agile mover.

DESCRIBED BY Young 1937
HABITAT Plains and woodland

large attachment points for jaw muscles

large eye sockets

turtlelike horny beak at front of mouth

broad toes on flat feet

Length: 6 ft (1.8 m)	Weight: ~220 lb (100 kg)	Diet: Tough vegetation, roots

Group: THERAPSIDA	Subgroup: Dicynodontia	Time: 255–250 mya

Lystrosaurus

LIS-TRO-SAW-RUS

Lystrosaurus, whose name means "shovel lizard," was a heavily built, early dicynodont with a short, stubby tail. It had two tusklike fangs made of horn. It used to be thought of as a type of reptilian hippopotamus because of its long, downturned snout and the placement of its nasal openings high on the snout. However, new analysis suggests a terrestrial lifestyle: the skull and jaw features were adaptations to a fibrous diet, the pelvis was well-developed, and the hind limbs were semierect.

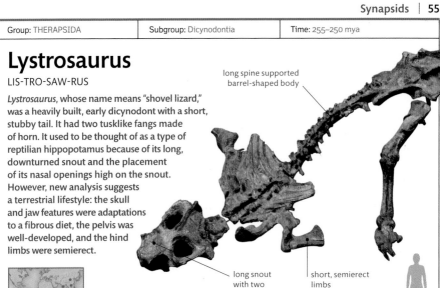

long spine supported barrel-shaped body

long snout with two horn fangs

short, semierect limbs

DESCRIBED BY Cope 1870
HABITAT Dry floodplains

Length: 3 ft (1 m)	Weight: ~200 lb (92 kg)	Diet: Plants

capacious ribcage held large mass of intestines

legs held in semisprawling gait

short legs

wide, barrel-shaped body

large limb girdles

Group: THERAPSIDA	Subgroup: Dicynodontia	Time: 220–216 mya

Placerias

PLAH-SEE-REE-AS

Placerias was a heavily built powerful animal, with the characteristic dicynodont jaw structure. Its jaw margins were toothless, except for two horny tusks near the front of the mouth. The tip of the snout ended in a beak used for uprooting plants. *Placerias* was one of the last of the dicynodont species.

DESCRIBED BY Lucas 1904
HABITAT Flood plains

bulky, heavily built body

horny tusks

short tail

flat, wide feet with four clawed toes

Length: 4–11 ft (1.2–3.5 m)	Weight: ~Up to 1 ton (1 metric ton)	Diet: Plants

Group: THERAPSIDA	Subgroup: Cynodontia	Time: 247–237 mya

Cynognathus

SY-NOG-NAY-THUS

This wolf-sized carnivore was a ferocious Triassic predator. It was one of the largest cynodonts ("dog-toothed" synapsids) and was heavily built, with strong legs positioned directly under its body and a tail shorter than that of most other reptiles. Its head was more than 12 in (30 cm) long. It is thought that it was probably endothermic, its skin may have been covered with hair, and it probably laid eggs. *Cynognathus* ("dog jaw") had doglike teeth, with cutting incisors, long canines, and a shearing set of cheek teeth. The jaws had a wide gape and a very powerful bite.

DESCRIBED BY Seeley 1895
HABITAT Woodland

large eye socket

Fossil skull

long canine teeth

Length: 5 ft (1.5 m)	Weight: ~88–110 lb (40–50 kg)	Diet: Herbivorous therapsids

Group: THERAPSIDA	Subgroup: Cynodontia	Time: 251–247 mya

Thrinaxodon
THRIN-AXE-OH-DON

This small, solidly built carnivore had a long body, which was distinctly divided into thoracic and lumbar regions (the first time this was seen among vertebrates). The division was marked by the ribs, which were borne only on the thoracic vertebrae. This suggests that *Thrinaxodon* ("trident tooth") probably had a diaphragm, as modern mammals do. One of the foot bones had evolved into a heel so that the foot could be levered clear of the ground for more efficient running. The teeth were set into a single bone, which made the jaws stronger.

DESCRIBED BY Seeley 1894
HABITAT Woodland

teeth with three sharp cusps

body may have been covered with hair

toes of equal length

Length: 20 in (50 cm)	Weight: Not calculated	Diet: Meat

Group: CYNODONTIA	Subgroup: Mammaliaformes	Time: 208–174 mya

Eozostrodon
EE-OH-ZOH-STROH-DON

This shrewlike animal was one of the earliest true mammals. It probably laid eggs, but it is thought to have fed its young with milk produced by mammary glands. Its four short legs had a slightly sprawling gait and ended in five-toed feet with claws. Its tail was long and possibly hairy. Its snout was long, slim, and contained true mammalian teeth. (The cheek teeth comprised simple premolars and molars with multiple sharp cusps and were replaced only once during the animal's lifetime.) The large eyes suggest that *Eozostrodon* was probably a nocturnal hunter, and the sharp teeth indicate a diet predominantly of insects and small animals. Recent analysis suggests that this genus is distinct from the later-named *Morganucodon*.

DESCRIBED BY Parrington 1941
HABITAT Forest floors

multicusped molars

Jaw bone

small body covered with dense hair

slim pointed snout may have had whiskers

large eyes

short legs

five clawed toes

Length: 4 in (10 cm)	Weight: ~5 oz (150 g)	Diet: Insects, small animals

JURASSIC PERIOD

201–145 MILLION YEARS AGO

AT THE BEGINNING of the Jurassic Period, the world was still hot and arid. Major continental movements caused climate change throughout the period: increased rainfall led to a reduction in desert areas; climates were more humid; and, as the period progressed, habitats in general became more green and lush. However, lake deposits show that there were millions of cycles of dry and wet periods. Most Jurassic plants were still mainly primitive types of gymnosperms. There were also ferns, horsetails, and club mosses, and huge forests of these plants spread worldwide. Continental movements led to the creation of warm, shallow seas, which became filled with coral reefs and new forms of marine life, including large reptiles. Pterosaurs were present in large numbers, and the earliest birds appeared at the end of the period.

JURASSIC LIFE

Early, bipedal sauropodomorphs still dominated Early Jurassic habitats, but as the period progressed, they were usurped by the giant sauropods, such as *Apatosaurus*. The first armored dinosaurs—the stegosaurs—also appeared. Protective armor may have been an evolutionary response to the emergence of ever-larger carnivorous dinosaurs. The first true mammals evolved and probably survived by remaining small and living a mainly nocturnal existence.

wing supported by greatly elongated fourth finger

relatively short tail

Marine predators
Giant pliosaurs, such as *Liopleurodon* (above), filled the warm Jurassic seas, hunting large prey, including other marine reptiles. They had developed an efficient "flying" action for swimming rapidly through the water.

Later pterosaurs
In the Late Jurassic, new forms of pterosaurs, such as *Anurognathus* (above), appeared. Their main feature was a very short tail that gave them greater agility in the air.

| 4,600 mya | 4,000 mya | 3,000 mya |

JURASSIC LANDMASSES

LAURASIA

TETHYS SEA

GONDWANA

At the start of the Jurassic Period, there was once again a supercontinent called Gondwana south of the Equator. Later in the period (see map), this split to form the landmasses that were to become present-day Australia, Antarctica, India, Africa, and South America. Laurasia (comprising the future North America and Europe) had begun to take shape in the northern hemisphere.

DIVERSITY

In the early Jurassic Period, the maximum size of dinosaurs increased, and this trend continued throughout the period. Because of this, mammals (such as *Sinoconodon*, below) and lizards tended to be rather small in order to maintain their ecological niches. In the seas, the ichthyosaurs, a fishlike group of marine reptiles, were at their zenith, sharing the warm Jurassic oceans with other marine predators, including plesiosaurs, sharks, and marine crocodiles.

Trees
Many forests of evergreen trees spread throughout the world. *Araucaria* were conifers. A fossilized cone is pictured, left.

2,000 mya   1,000 mya   500 mya   250 mya   0

THEROPODS

THE JURASSIC saw the true transition to dinosaur-dominated ecosystems, and theropods replaced pseudosuchians as top predators. Some of the early lineages, like dilophosaurids, became slightly larger, but it was the ceratosaurs and tetanurans that dominated the food chain. The ceratosaur lineage spawned the abelisaurs, which remained top predators in the southern hemisphere until the end-Cretaceous extinction. Tetanurans diverged in skull shape, with some groups developing elaborate crests and horns, and others an elongated snout—taken to an extreme in the bizarre spinosaurs.

As these lineages were getting bigger, other groups like the coelurosaurs were getting smaller, so theropods occupied a wide variety of ecological roles. Many of the lineages that would come to rule the Cretaceous originated in the Jurassic, including dromaeosaurs, tyrannosaurs, and troodontids. Some of these coelurosaurs, which were fast runners with relatively long arms, started to use their feathered forelimbs in unique ways, experimenting with generating lift by flapping or gliding. It is now clear that active powered flight originated independently multiple times in these dinosaurs, but one particular dinosaur, *Archaeopteryx* (see pp.70–71), was especially adept at flying. Its relatives continue to rule the skies today.

Group: THEROPODA	Subgroup: Ceratosauria	Time: 156–149 mya

Ceratosaurus

SER-AT-OH-SAW-RUS

Ceratosaurus ("horned lizard") was named for the short horn above its nose. Another striking feature was the line of bony plates that ran down its back—so far, it is the only theropod known to have had them. It had strong yet short arms, with four fingers on each hand. Three of the fingers were clawed. It had a deep, broad tail, and feet with three large toes and a reduced back toe. Its teeth were long and bladelike. Although it superficially resembled a carnosaur such as *Allosaurus*, it was more primitive, and its tail was flexible rather than stiffened with bony ligaments as was the case with the carnosaurs.

DESCRIBED BY Marsh 1884
HABITAT Forested plains

light skull

body balanced
at hips

saurischian
hip structure

three long,
forward-facing,
clawed toes

Length: 15–20 ft (4.5–6 m)	Weight: ~1 ton (1 metric ton)	Diet: Herbivorous dinosaurs, other reptiles

Group: THEROPODA	Subgroup: Dilophosauridae	Time: 199–182 mya

Dilophosaurus

DI-LOAF-OH-SAW-RUS

Dilophosaurus ("two-ridged lizard") was named for the striking pair of bony crests that adorned its head. These were so thin and fragile that they were almost certainly only used for sexual display. *Dilophosaurus* had a more primitive body structure than that of coelurosaurs and carnosaurs—it had a large head but was lightly built, with a slender neck, body, and tail. Once thought to have been closely related to *Coelophysis* for its four-fingered hand and a notch in its upper jaw, it is now more likely to be somewhat intermediate between *Coelophysis* and the larger Ceratosaurs.

DESCRIBED BY Welles 1970
HABITAT Riverbanks

bony, semicircular crests

three long, forward-facing, clawed toes

flexible tail

long, slim, powerful hind legs

Length: 20 ft (6 m)	Weight: ~½ ton (500 kg)	Diet: Small animals, possibly fish or carrion

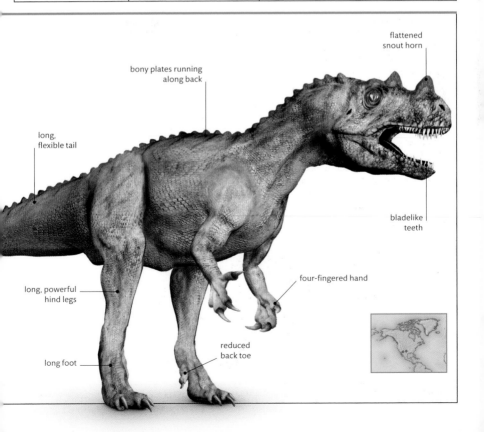

flattened snout horn

bony plates running along back

long, flexible tail

long, powerful hind legs

four-fingered hand

bladelike teeth

long foot

reduced back toe

Group: THEROPODA	Subgroup: Tetanurae	Time: 171–161 mya

Gasosaurus

GAS-OH-SAW-RUS

This theropod was given its unusual name ("gas lizard") in honor of the Chinese gas-mining company that was working in the quarry where the fossil remains were excavated. The single species *Gasosaurus constructus* is represented by a single specimen. Remains included a humerus, the pelvis, and a femur. Little is known about *Gasosaurus*, and its classification is still uncertain. It may be a primitive carnosaur; however, some features of the leg bones suggest that it may be an early coelurosaur instead. If so, it would be one of the oldest coelurosaurs so far discovered. *Gasosaurus* had the typical theropod body shape of a large head; long, powerful legs ending in three forward-facing clawed toes; and a long, stiff tail. It had very short arms, but they were longer than those of later carnosaurs.

large jaws with sharp teeth

DESCRIBED BY
Dong and Tang 1985
HABITAT Woodland.

Length: 10 ft (3.1 m)	Weight: ~330 lb (150 kg)	Diet: Large herbivorous dinosaurs

Group: CARNOSAURIA	Subgroup: Allosauroidea	Time: 166–163 mya

Piatnitzkysaurus

PEAT-NYITS-KEE-SAW-RUS

Piatnitzkysaurus, whose name means "Piatnitzky lizard," seems to have been a tetanuran (stiff-tailed) theropod. Two partial skeletons have been excavated to date, and its exact classification is still under debate by paleontologists. It had a very similar body to *Allosaurus* (see p.64), but its arms were longer. Its head was large and was carried on a short, muscular neck. The arms were relatively small. The body was bulky, and the tail was long and stiff.

DESCRIBED BY
Bonaparte 1979
HABITAT Woodland

short, powerful arms

Length: 14 ft (4.3 m)	Weight: ~880 lb (400 kg)	Diet: Herbivorous dinosaurs

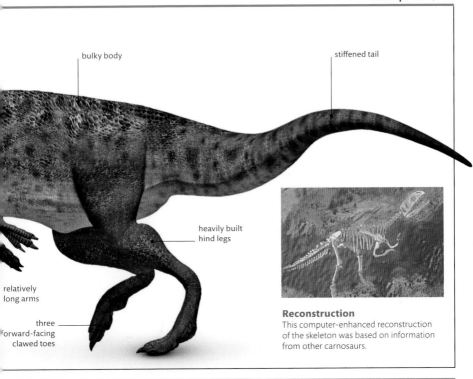

bulky body

stiffened tail

heavily built
hind legs

relatively
long arms

three
forward-facing
clawed toes

Reconstruction
This computer-enhanced reconstruction
of the skeleton was based on information
from other carnosaurs.

Group: CARNOSAURIA	Subgroup: Megalosauridae	Time: 166 mya

Megalosaurus

MEG-A-LOH-SAW-RUS

The first dinosaur to be scientifically named
and identified, *Megalosaurus* ("great lizard")
was a large, bulky, carnivorous theropod.
It had a massive head carried on a short,
muscular neck. Its arms were short but
strong. Fossil trackways found in southern
England show how *Megalosaurus* walked
with its toes pointing slightly inward, with
its tail probably swinging from side to side
for balance.

DESCRIBED BY Buckland 1824
HABITAT Forests

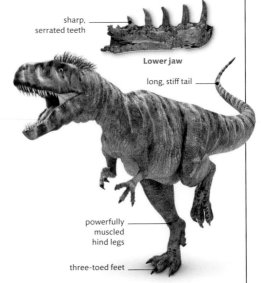

sharp,
serrated teeth

Lower jaw

long, stiff tail

powerfully
muscled
hind legs

three-toed feet

Length: 30 ft (9 m)	Weight: ~1–2 tons (1–2 metric tons)	Diet: Large herbivorous dinosaurs

Group: CARNOSAURIA	Subgroup: Allosauroidea	Time: 156–149 mya

Allosaurus

AL-OH-SAW-RUS

Allosaurus ("different lizard") was the most abundant, and probably the largest, predator in the late Jurassic Period in the lands that were to become North America. It was typical of its family of meat-eating dinosaurs, with a massive head, short neck, and bulky body. Its tail was long and deep, with a thin, stiff end. Its three-fingered forelimbs were strong, with large claws. *Allosaurus* had distinctive bony bumps over the eyes and a narrow ridge of bone running between them down to the tip of the snout. These features may have been used for display. Although the head was massive, it was lightened by several large openings (fenestrae) between the bones. Expandable joints between the skull bones allowed the jaws to gape open sideways to swallow large mouthfuls. Despite its large size and lack of speed, some paleontologists believe that *Allosaurus* was agile enough to fell the giant plant-eating dinosaurs of the time.

DESCRIBED BY
Marsh 1877
HABITAT Plains

distinctive ridge of bone along snout

teeth with serrated front and back edges

FOSSIL FINDS

Many complete skeletons of *Allosaurus* have been excavated. Many partial skeletons have been found in the Cleveland-Lloyd Dinosaur Quarry in Utah. This site is thought to have been a place where herbivorous dinosaurs became stuck in mud and attracted predators, which also became trapped as they attacked the helpless prey.

tail held outstretched for balance

Othniel C. Marsh
One of the greatest dinosaur paleontologists of the 19th century, Othniel C. Marsh, described *Allosaurus* and more than 500 other vertebrates.

Length: 39 ft (12 m)	Weight: ~2–3 tons (2–3 metric tons)	Diet: Herbivorous dinosaurs, carrion

massive skull lightened by
large fenestrae (openings)

large attachment
points for powerful
jaw muscles

2½–5-in
(5–10-cm)
long teeth

bladelike teeth
for slicing

Fossil skull

powerful upper
jaw had an
axlike action

| Group: CARNOSAURIA | Subgroup: Allosauroidea | Time: 161–159 mya |

Sinraptor

SINE-RAP-TOR

Sinraptor ("Chinese thief") was part
of the lineage that led to *Allosaurus*.
Although it was more primitive, it had
more specializations for its role as an
apex predator than earlier relatives such as
Megalosaurus. Its teeth were highly adapted for
a carnivorous lifestyle: durable teeth at the front of the
mouth were adapted for a bone-crunching bite, and
the other teeth would have ripped through flesh to cause
deep wounds. *Sinraptor* probably used these adaptations
to take down giant sauropods, such as *Mamenchisaurus*
(see p.77), that it lived alongside.

many sharp teeth

DESCRIBED BY Currie and Zhao 1993
HABITAT Marshland

clawed hands

| Length: 23¼ ft (7.2 m) | Weight: ~1 ton (1 metric ton) | Diet: Meat |

| Group: TETANURAE | Subgroup: Coelurosauria | Time: 153–149 mya |

Ornitholestes

OR-NITH-OH-LESS-TEES

Ornitholestes ("bird robber") was a slim, lightly
built dinosaur, with a small head, many conical
teeth, and an S-shaped neck. A long, tapering
tail contributed to
greater agility
when running.
Its name arose
because its grasping
hands, light build, and
long hindlimbs made it an efficient
hunter of small Jurassic animals. Its arms were
short and strong; its hands had three long,
clawed fingers. An additional finger was very
small. *Ornitholestes* had many birdlike features,
and its wrist structure allowed it to tuck
its hands up close to its body in the same
manner that a bird folds its wings.

long, flexible neck

birdlike
clawed feet

three long and
one short finger
on each hand

DESCRIBED BY
Osborn 1903
HABITAT Forests

| Length: 6½ ft (2 m) | Weight: ~26 lb (12 kg) | Diet: Meat, possibly including birds, carrion |

strong,
thick tail

long, powerful legs

very long, thin,
tapering tail

tail held
outstretched

body balanced
at hip

Fossil-hunting expedition
Leading US paleontologist Henry
F. Osborn (1857–1935) undertook
many fossil-hunting expeditions in
Mongolia and the US in the 1900s.

Group: COELUROSAURIA	Subgroup: Compsognathidae	Time: 150 mya

Compsognathus

COMP-SOG-NAY-THUS

slim, pointed head and snout

relatively large eyes

This theropod, whose name means "pretty jaw," was about the size of a modern turkey. Its skeletal structure shows that it must have been a fast runner—its bones were hollow, its shins were much longer than its thighs, and its long tail was held outstretched for balance. Its arms were short, probably with three fingers. Its feet were very birdlike, with three clawed toes facing forward. *Compsognathus* was anatomically very similar to *Archaeopteryx* (pp.70-71), with the exception of wings, and lived in similar areas. The presence of primitive feathers on a closely related genus—*Sinosauropteryx*—suggests that *Compsognathus* could also have had a downy body covering, although there is no direct evidence for this.

DESCRIBED BY Wagner 1861
HABITAT Warm, moist areas and brush

ADULT REMAINS

Only two skeletons of *Compsognathus* have been found—an adult and a juvenile specimen. Both were found with a skeleton inside their stomach. At first, it was thought that the remains were of a fetus, but it turned out to be a lizard (*Bavarisaurus*).

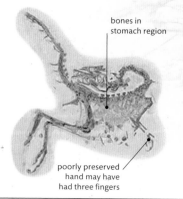

bones in stomach region

poorly preserved hand may have had three fingers

Length: 3 ft (1 m)	Weight: ~6½ lb (3 kg)	Diet: Small lizards, mammals

lightweight body
balanced at hips

tail held stiffly
out for balance

slim, short
thighs

Group: PARAVES	Subgroup: Avialae	Time: 150 mya

Archaeopteryx

ARE-KAY-OP-TER-IKS

Archaeopteryx ("ancient wing") was about the size of a modern pigeon, with a small head, large eyes, and pointed teeth in its jaws. Its lower leg bones were long and slim, indicating that it could move well on land. Unlike modern birds, *Archaeopteryx* had a flat breastbone; a long, bony tail; and three grasping claws on each wing. However, its feathers, wings, and furcula (wishbone) are characteristics shared by modern birds. Recent analysis shows that *Archaeopteryx* could probably fly, although it may not have been a strong flier. It was almost certainly endothermic.

DESCRIBED BY von Meyer 1861

HABITAT Lakeshores or open forests

three clawed digits on elongated hand

feathered wings for effective flight

lightly built body

Length: 12 in (30 cm)	Weight: ~11–18 oz (300–500 g)	Diet: Insects

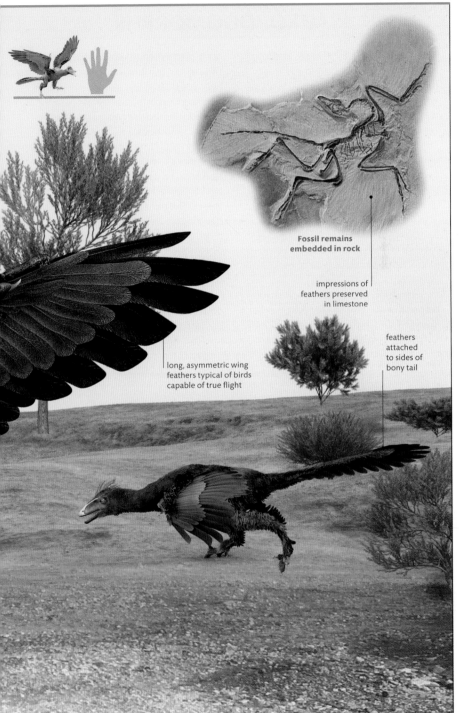

**Fossil remains
embedded in rock**

impressions of
feathers preserved
in limestone

long, asymmetric wing
feathers typical of birds
capable of true flight

feathers
attached
to sides of
bony tail

SAUROPODOMORPHS

THROUGHOUT THE TRIASSIC and into the Jurassic, sauropodomorphs were transitioning to a quadrupedal stance and had adopted a strictly herbivorous diet. These two features enabled them to reach much larger body sizes after the Triassic-Jurassic extinction. Some of these early Jurassic species were enormous, such as *Ledumahadi*, which at 13.2 tons (12 metric tons) would have been the largest land animal ever at that time.

In the early Jurassic, the first true sauropods appeared, distinguished by their pillarlike legs and long necks with tiny heads. Sauropods would become incredibly successful in the Jurassic, radiating around the globe and reaching truly astonishing sizes. Three main groups diverged, and each developed a unique body plan, which allowed them to coexist throughout the Jurassic. The diplodocids had elongated necks and tails, and were able to grow to incredibly large sizes. Diplodocids include some of the best-known sauropods, such as *Apatosaurus* and the recently resurrected *Brontosaurus*. Their close cousins, the dicraeosaurs, remained relatively small and had shorter necks adorned with two rows of tall spines. The third group, the macronarians, had longer forelimbs that gave them a more upright stance, as exemplified by *Giraffatitan* (see pp.80–81). Macronarians, named for their large nostrils, varied in size, with some subgroups, such as camarasaurids, remaining small, and others, such as the brachiosaurids and later titanosaurians, becoming much larger.

Group: SAUROPODOMORPHA	Subgroup: Massospondylidae	Time: 201–182 mya

Massospondylus

MASS-OH-SPON-DI-LUSS

Massospondylus ("massive vertebrae") was named for the first remains found—a few large vertebrae. Many fossil finds have now been made, and it appears to have been the most common sauropodomorph in what is now southern Africa. *Massospondylus* had a tiny head on a long, flexible neck. It was previously thought to have spent most of its time on all fours, but recent analysis suggests that *Massospondylus* moved around on its hind legs. It had massive, five-fingered hands that could be used for holding food. Each thumb had a large, curved claw. The front teeth were rounded, and the back ones had flat sides, indicating a tough plant diet. Gizzard stones have been found with some skeletons.

deep spines under tail vertebrae

long tail with thin, whiplash end

DESCRIBED BY Owen 1854
HABITAT Shrubland and desert plains

Length: 13 ft (4 m)	Weight: ~330 lb (150 kg)		Diet: Plants, possibly small animals

Group: SAURISCHIA	Subgroup: Sauropodomorpha	Time: 201–190 mya

Anchisaurus

AN-CHEE-SAW-RUS

Anchisaurus was an early sauropodomorph. It had a small head with a narrow snout; a long, flexible neck; and a slim body and tail. Although its arms were a third shorter than its legs, it spent most of its time on all fours. The thumbs had a large claw that may have been used for defense.

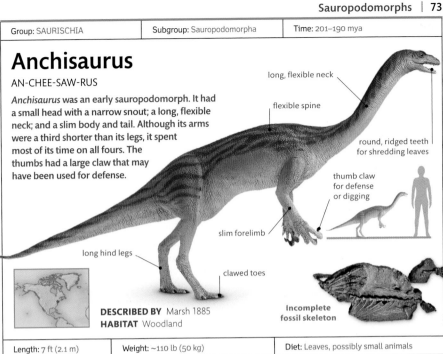

long, flexible neck

flexible spine

round, ridged teeth for shredding leaves

thumb claw for defense or digging

slim forelimb

long hind legs

clawed toes

DESCRIBED BY Marsh 1885
HABITAT Woodland

Incomplete fossil skeleton

Length: 7 ft (2.1 m)	Weight: ~110 lb (50 kg)	Diet: Leaves, possibly small animals

sharp end used for digging or defense

large, curved claw

Fossil thumb claw

hands with massive span

extremely long, flexible neck

Group: SAUROPODOMORPHA	Subgroup: Massospondylidae	Time: 201–190 mya

Lufengosaurus

LOO-FUNG-OH-SAW-RUS

Lufengosaurus ("lizard from Lufeng") was a heavy, stout-limbed sauropodomorph. Its small head held many widely spaced teeth that were shaped like leaves, a typical feature of sauropodomorph dinosaurs. Its lower jaw was hinged below the level of the upper teeth. This gave the jaw muscles greater leverage for feeding on tough plant material. Its broad feet had four long toes, and its large hands had long, clawed fingers; the thumbs bore a massive claw. *Lufengosaurus* would have moved around on its hind legs, sometimes rearing up and stretching out its long neck to feed on cycad or conifer trees.

DESCRIBED BY Young 1940
HABITAT Desert plains

relatively large, deep head

paired pubic bones projected back

bulky, heavy body

hands with large span

Length: 20 ft (6 m)	Weight: ~1–3¼ tons (1–3 metric tons)	Diet: Cycad and conifer leaves

Group: SAUROPODOMORPHA	Subgroup: Sauropoda	Time: 199–182 mya

Barapasaurus

BA-RAP-A-SAW-RUS

Barapasaurus ("big-legged lizard") is one of the earliest known sauropods. There is fossil evidence for all parts of the skeleton, with the exception of the skull and feet, making it potentially the best-known Early Jurassic sauropod. However, to date it still has not been fully described, and its provisional classification may change in the light of future findings. *Barapasaurus* had slim limbs; spoon-shaped, saw-edged teeth (found in isolation); and unusual hollows in the vertebrae of the back. Paleontologists believe this dinosaur had a short, deep head, like skulls from other primitive sauropods.

DESCRIBED BY Jain et al. 1975
HABITAT Plains

long, flexible tail

Length: 60 ft (18 m)	Weight: ~22 tons (20 metric tons)	Diet: Plants

Group: SAUROPODOMORPHA	Subgroup: Sauropoda	Time: 159 mya

Shunosaurus

SHOON-OH-SAW-RUS

Nearly complete skeletons of *Shunosaurus* ("Shu lizard") have been discovered, and it was only the second sauropod to be known in its entirety. The skull is long and low, with small teeth. A surprising feature is the small, bony club at the end of its tail formed by enlarged vertebrae (not seen in the pictured specimen).

DESCRIBED BY
Dong et al. 1983
HABITAT Plains

low head with large nostrils

long, flexible neck

relatively short forelegs

Length: 33 ft (10 m)	Weight: ~11 tons (10 metric tons)	Diet: Plants

heavy, bulky body

neck made up of long vertebrae

elephantlike legs and feet

Group: SAUROPODA	Subgroup: Diplodocidae	Time: 152–150 mya

Barosaurus

BA-ROH-SAW-RUS

Barosaurus ("heavy lizard") had all the typical features of its family—a long neck and tail, bulky body, tiny head, and relatively short legs for its size. Its limbs are indistinguishable from those of *Diplodocus* (see p.78), but its neck was much longer. Its 15 cervical vertebrae were greatly elongated—a third longer than in *Diplodocus*. *Barosaurus* probably roamed in herds and relied on its huge size for defense against the large predators of the time.

DESCRIBED BY Marsh 1890
HABITAT Floodplains

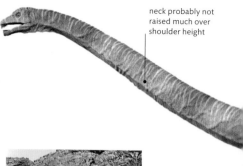

neck probably not raised much over shoulder height

Dinosaur hunting
The camp at Carnegie Quarry, Utah, where three *Barosaurus* skeletons were found in 1922.

Length: 75–89 ft (23–27 m)	Weight: ~20 tons (19⅝ metric tons)	Diet: Plants

Group: SAUROPODOMORPHA	Subgroup: Sauropoda	Time: 168–166 mya

Cetiosaurus

SEE-TEE-OH-SAW-RUS

This dinosaur, whose name means "whale lizard," was discovered early in the 18th century. Its huge bones were thought to belong to some type of immense whale—hence its name. It was a large, heavy sauropod with a shorter neck and tail than other sauropods. It was also different in that its vertebrae had fewer hollow spaces to lighten them than other sauropods of its size. Its head was blunt and contained spoon-shaped teeth. *Cetiosaurus* is thought to have roamed in large herds at an estimated walking speed of 10 mph (15 kph).

DESCRIBED BY Owen 1841
HABITAT Plains

solid centrum of vertebra

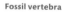

Fossil vertebra

tail held outstretched in life

5-ft (1.5-m) long shoulder blade (mounted too vertically in this reconstruction)

Length: 59 ft (18 m)	Weight: ~8⅞ tons (9 metric tons)	Diet: Plants

powerful tail with
whiplash end

elongated
vertebra of
the back

front legs
shorter than
hind legs

elephantlike
limbs

Vertebra

Group: SAUROPODOMORPHA	Subgroup: Sauropoda	Time: 152–114 mya

Mamenchisaurus

MAH-MEN-CHI-SAW-RUS

This dinosaur, whose name means "Mamenxi lizard," had one of
the longest necks of any dinosaur. It made up more than half of the
animal's total length and contained 19 vertebrae—more than any
other dinosaur. The neck vertebrae were over twice the length of
those in its back and were overlapped by long, thin, bony struts.
It is thought that this restricted movement to the joint between the
head and the uppermost neck bone, with the dinosaur holding its
neck not much higher than shoulder height. It could then swing
it widely from the shoulders to browse
on low vegetation.

Fossil remains
Remains of *Mamenchisaurus*
have been excavated from
sites in China.

DESCRIBED BY
Young 1954
HABITAT Deltas
and forested areas

enormously
elongated
neck

back sloping
from shoulders

Length: 114 ft (35 m)	Weight: ~66 tons (60 metric tons)	Diet: Leaves and shoots

| Group: SAUROPODA | Subgroup: Diplodocidae | Time: 154–152 mya |

Diplodocus
DIPLOH-DOCK-US

Diplodocus was one of the longest dinosaurs. It was lightly built, with slim limbs and a tapered tail with a whiplash end. Its name, meaning "double beam," comes from the chevron bones under its tail vertebrae. There are three species of *Diplodocus*: *D. longus*, *D. carnegii*, and *D. hallorum*.

peglike teeth at front of jaws

DESCRIBED BY
Marsh 1878
HABITAT Plains

| Length: 104 ft (32 m) | Weight: ~22 tons (20 metric tons) | Diet: Leaves |

| Group: SAUROPODA | Subgroup: Macronaria | Time: 156–149 mya |

Camarasaurus
CAM-A-RAH-SAW-RUS

Camarasaurus ("chambered lizard") was the most common sauropod in North America. It appears to have roamed in large herds. This dinosaur had a relatively large, box-shaped head and short neck and tail. The vertebrae probably contained air spaces to lighten the backbone. The front legs of *Camarasaurus* were relatively long. Its forefeet had one single claw and the hind feet three.

DESCRIBED BY Cope 1877
HABITAT Plains

| Length: 75 ft (23 m) | Weight: ~51 tons (47 metric tons) | Diet: Tough vegetation |

Group: SAUROPODA	Subgroup: Diplodocidae	Time: 152–151 mya

Apatosaurus
A-PAT-OH-SAW-RUS

Apatosaurus was shorter yet heavier and bulkier than its close relatives. It had a tiny head at the end of a long neck made up of 15 vertebrae. Its back vertebrae were hollow, and its long tail had a whiplike end. Its thick hind legs were longer than the front ones, possibly to allow the dinosaur to rear up when feeding. Whether *Apatosaurus* could actually do this is disputed by some paleontologists.

DESCRIBED BY Marsh 1877
HABITAT Wooded plains

tail comprising over half the total length

neck with limited mobility

relatively short front legs

Length: 70 ft (21 m)	Weight: ~42 tons (37 metric tons)	Diet: Leaves

massive, heavy body

short head

nasal chambers high on snout

single claw on front feet

Fossil skull

Group: SAUROPODA	Subgroup: Macronaria	Time: 157–145 mya

Giraffatitan

JI-RAF-A-TIE-TAN

Giraffatitan is known from all parts of the skeleton except for the important neural arches of the vertebrae at the base of the neck. It was one of the tallest and largest sauropods and the one in which the lengthening of the forelimbs relative to the hindlimbs reached its extreme. Together with its long neck, ending in a small head, *Giraffatitan*'s giraffelike stance gave it a great height: up to 50 ft (16 m). The tail was relatively short and thick. Like other members of its family, *Giraffatitan* had chisel-like teeth—26 on each jaw—toward the front of the mouth. The nostrils were at the front of the snout and soft tissue ran back to the nostril openings in the skull. The legs were pillarlike and the feet all had five toes with fleshy pads behind. The first toe of each front foot bore a claw, as did the first three toes of the hind feet. Like other sauropods, it probably traveled in herds. *Giraffatitan* was adapted for feeding off vegetation from the tops of trees. The length of its neck means that it would have had to have an extremely large, powerful heart and very high blood pressure to pump blood up to its head. *Giraffatitan* is thought to have laid its eggs while walking, leaving the young to fend for themselves.

DESCRIBED BY Janensch 1914
HABITAT Plains

MASSIVE BONES

The femur (thigh bone) of the closely related *Brachiosaurus* was over 6 ft (1.8 m) long and massively thick to support the dinosaur's weight. One of the first bones discovered by Elmer S. Riggs, in 1900, was the humerus (upper arm bone). It was over 7 ft (2.1 m) long, which was so much greater than that of any known humerus that Riggs thought it was a crushed femur of an *Apatosaurus* (see p.79).

ball-like head of femur

body sloping downward from shoulder to hip

short tail

relatively slim, pillarlike legs

Length: 85 ft (26 m)	Weight: ~49½ tons (50 metric tons)	Diet: Plants

chisel-like teeth
at front of mouth

long neck made
up of 3-ft (1-m)
long vertebrae

air sacs in
the vertebrae
lightened the neck

forelimbs longer
than hindlimbs

ORNITHISCHIANS

THE ORIGINS of the herbivorous ornithischians are still a mystery. There are no definitive records prior to the Jurassic, even though they should have branched off from other dinosaurs during the Late Triassic.

Ornithischians had a toothless, bony beak at the front of the mouth, and cheeks that would have held food as it was ground by specialized teeth. Two lineages of ornithischians are known from the early part of the Jurassic: the armored thyreophorans and the agile, bipedal cerapodans. Early thyreophorans, such as *Scutellosaurus*, were bipedal, but the group would soon become quadrupedal and split into the plate-backed stegosaurs and heavily armored ankylosaurs. Throughout the Jurassic these two groups shared the role of large herbivores with the sauropods, although they relied on their armor and weaponized tails for protection rather than reaching the enormous sizes of sauropods.

The exact relationships of early cerapodans are still being untangled, but by the Middle Jurassic, representatives of both lineages—marginocephalians and ornithopods—were known. The marginocephalians—named for the extended margin protruding from the back of their skull, would give rise to frilled ceratopsians and dome-headed pachycephalosaurs. For most of the Jurassic, ornithopods remained small, quick, bipedal runners, but some started to get larger later—foreshadowing the rise of hadrosaurs and iguanodontians in the Cretaceous.

Group: DINOSAURIA	Subgroup: Ornithischia	Time: 201–190 mya

Lesothosaurus

LE-SOO-TOE-SAW-RUS

Lesothosaurus ("Lesotho lizard") was an early bipedal herbivorous dinosaur. It was small and built for speed, with a lightly built body; long, slim legs; and a thin, flexible tail. It had pointed front teeth; serrated, arrow-shaped cheek teeth; and jaws that moved only up and down, not from side to side. *Lesothosaurus* had a limited ability to chew its food, and most of the food processing was done with its beak. It may have been an omnivore.

DESCRIBED BY Galton 1978
HABITAT Desert plains

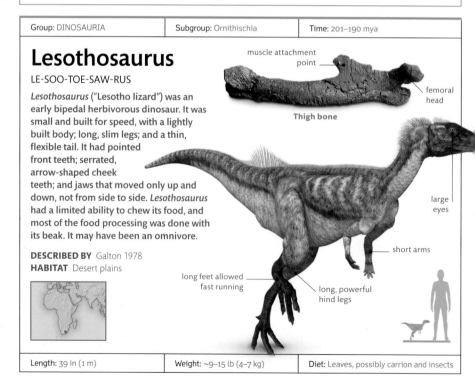

muscle attachment point

femoral head

Thigh bone

large eyes

short arms

long feet allowed fast running

long, powerful hind legs

Length: 39 in (1 m)	Weight: ~9–15 lb (4–7 kg)	Diet: Leaves, possibly carrion and insects

Group: ORNITHISCHIA	Subgroup: Thyreophora	Time: 199–190 mya

Scutellosaurus

SCOO-TELL-OH-SAW-RUS

This "little shield lizard" had a long body and slim limbs. Its arms were also relatively long and slender. Over 300 low, bony studs covered its back, flanks, and the base of its tail to form a defensive armor. Recent analysis suggests that *Scutellosaurus* spent most of its time on its hind legs, holding its tail stiffly out behind it to counterbalance the weight of the bony armor.

DESCRIBED BY Colbert 1981
HABITAT Woodland

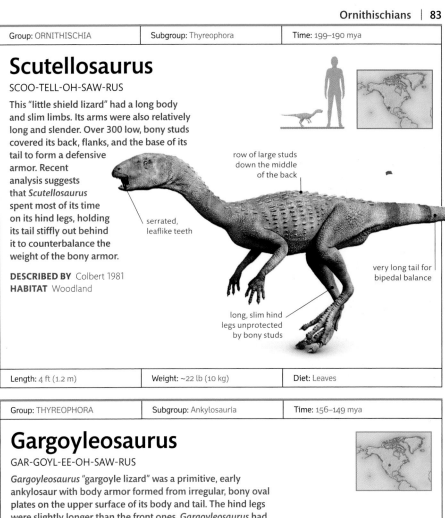

row of large studs down the middle of the back

serrated, leaflike teeth

very long tail for bipedal balance

long, slim hind legs unprotected by bony studs

Length: 4 ft (1.2 m)	Weight: ~22 lb (10 kg)	Diet: Leaves

Group: THYREOPHORA	Subgroup: Ankylosauria	Time: 156–149 mya

Gargoyleosaurus

GAR-GOYL-EE-OH-SAW-RUS

Gargoyleosaurus "gargole lizard" was a primitive, early ankylosaur with body armor formed from irregular, bony oval plates on the upper surface of its body and tail. The hind legs were slightly longer than the front ones. *Gargoyleosaurus* had many features unusual among ankylosaurs, including a straight nasal passage and hollow armor plates. The skull shows features seen in late Cretaceous ankylosaurs, including fusion of bone armor to the surface of the skull and jaw.

DESCRIBED BY Carpenter et al. 1998
HABITAT Woodland

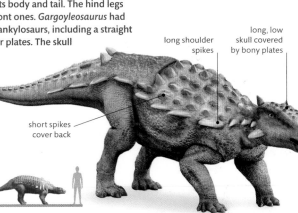

long shoulder spikes

long, low skull covered by bony plates

short spikes cover back

Length: 10 ft (3 m)	Weight: ~1 ton (1 metric ton)	Diet: Low-lying vegetation

Group: ORNITHISCHIA	Subgroup: Thyreophora	Time: 199–182 mya

Scelidosaurus

SCEL-EYE-DOH-SAW-RUS

This small, heavy, armored dinosaur, whose name means "limb lizard," seems to be one of the earliest and most primitive thyreophorans. Recent research suggests that it was a primitive ankylosaur. It had impressive defensive armor: its back was covered with bony plates and studded with a double row of bony spikes. Additional rows of studs ran along its sides, and there was a pair of triple-spiked bony plates behind the neck. The head was small and pointed, with a horny beak and small, leaf-shaped teeth. Although the forelimbs were much shorter than the hindlimbs, *Scelidosaurus* seems to have walked on all fours.

underside of tail covered by bony studs

three long and one short, clawed digits

DESCRIBED BY
Owen 1861
HABITAT Woodland

longer feet than later thyreophorans

Fossil foot

Length: 11 ft (3.5 m)	Weight: ~550 lb (250 kg)	Diet: Plants

Group: THYREOPHORA	Subgroup: Stegosauria	Time: 156–150 mya

Kentrosaurus

KEN-TRO-SAW-RUS

This East African contemporary of *Stegosaurus* was smaller than its more famous relative but just as well protected. *Kentrosaurus* ("spiked lizard") had paired rectangular plates running down over the neck, shoulders, and half of the back. Over the hips, the plates gave way to sharp spikes, which ran in pairs down to the tip of the tail. Another pair of long spikes jutted out from the hips on each side. The skull is known only from fragments, but it was probably long and slender, with a toothless, horny beak.

DESCRIBED BY Hennig 1915
HABITAT Forests

pairs of sharp spikes from mid back to tail tip

Length: 16 ft (5 m)	Weight: ~1⅔ tons (1.5 metric tons)	Diet: Low-lying vegetation

parallel rows of
bony studs running
down the back

triple-spiked
bony plate

hips
higher
than
shoulders

horny beak
for nipping
at plants

strong
hind legs

paired bony plates
running down neck
and upper back

large body cavity

small,
sloping
head

relatively long,
sturdily built
hind legs

forelegs much shorter
than hind legs for
low browsing

Group: THYREOPHORA	Subgroup: Stegosauria	Time: 156–149 mya

Stegosaurus
STEG-OH-SAW-RUS

Stegosaurus ("roof lizard") was the largest plated dinosaur. It had a tiny head, toothless beak, and two rows of bony plates running from behind its neck to halfway along its tail. Some of these plates were over 24 in (60 cm) high. The tail also had long spikes, each up to 39 in (1 m) long, the number of which varied between species. The dinosaur's neck was also armored with many tiny bony studs. The hind legs were twice as long as the forelegs, meaning that the body's highest point was at the hips. *Stegosaurus* had a toothless beak and small cheek teeth that could not chew, so exactly how *Stegosaurus* processed enough vegetation to survive remains unclear.

DESCRIBED BY Marsh 1877
HABITAT Woodland

covering of skin or tough horn over plates

massive body

Length: 20 ft (6 m)	Weight: ~2 tons (2 metric tons)	Diet: Plants

long spines on
tail vertebrae

Skeletal reconstruction

plates graduated in
size along the tail

tail spikes varied
in number
between species

PLATES AND SPIKES

Some early reconstructions of *Stegosaurus*
have the plates arranged in pairs. Scientists have
revised their reconstructions over time to put
them in a zigzag pattern.

pointed tip

very sharp,
bony tail
spikes

Fossil plate

**Fossil tail
spike**

Group: ORNITHISCHIA	Subgroup: Heterodontosauridae	Time: 201–190 mya

Heterodontosaurus

HET-ER-OH-DONT-OH-SAW-RUS

As its name ("different-toothed lizard") suggests, the most remarkable feature of this small bipedal dinosaur was its teeth. *Heterodontosaurus* had three kinds: cutting incisors at the front of the upper jaw, two pairs of large tusklike teeth, and tall chisel-like teeth used for shredding vegetation. The tusks may have been used for defense, sexual display, or feeding.

cutting incisors

shredding cheek teeth

Fossil skull

DESCRIBED BY Crompton and Charig 1962
HABITAT Shrubland

bony rods stiffened back and tail

horny beak

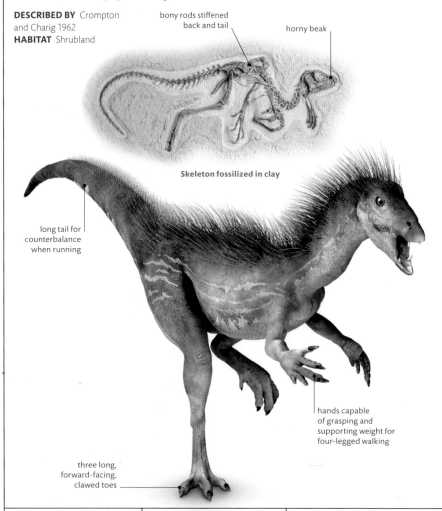

Skeleton fossilized in clay

long tail for counterbalance when running

hands capable of grasping and supporting weight for four-legged walking

three long, forward-facing, clawed toes

Length: 4 ft (1.2 m)	Weight: ~42 lb (19 kg)	Diet: Leaves, tubers, possibly insects

| Group: ORNITHOPODA | Subgroup: Iguanodontia | Time: 156–149 mya |

Dryosaurus
DRY-OH-SAW-RUS

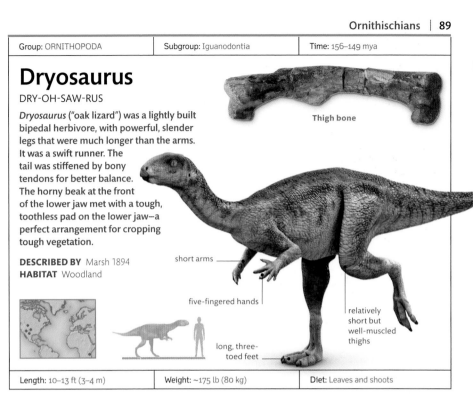

Thigh bone

Dryosaurus ("oak lizard") was a lightly built bipedal herbivore, with powerful, slender legs that were much longer than the arms. It was a swift runner. The tail was stiffened by bony tendons for better balance. The horny beak at the front of the lower jaw met with a tough, toothless pad on the lower jaw—a perfect arrangement for cropping tough vegetation.

DESCRIBED BY Marsh 1894
HABITAT Woodland

short arms

five-fingered hands

relatively short but well-muscled thighs

long, three-toed feet

| Length: 10–13 ft (3–4 m) | Weight: ~175 lb (80 kg) | Diet: Leaves and shoots |

| Group: ORNITHOPODA | Subgroup: Iguanodontia | Time: 156–149 mya |

Camptosaurus
KAMP-TOE-SAW-RUS

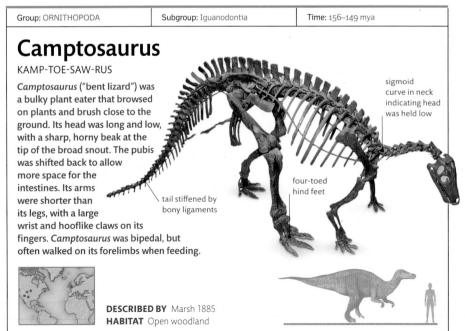

Camptosaurus ("bent lizard") was a bulky plant eater that browsed on plants and brush close to the ground. Its head was long and low, with a sharp, horny beak at the tip of the broad snout. The pubis was shifted back to allow more space for the intestines. Its arms were shorter than its legs, with a large wrist and hooflike claws on its fingers. *Camptosaurus* was bipedal, but often walked on its forelimbs when feeding.

sigmoid curve in neck indicating head was held low

four-toed hind feet

tail stiffened by bony ligaments

DESCRIBED BY Marsh 1885
HABITAT Open woodland

| Length: 16–23 ft (5–7 m) | Weight: ~¾ ton (750 kg) | Diet: Low-growing herbs and brush |

OTHER DIAPSIDS

ALTHOUGH DINOSAURS ruled the Jurassic lands, their diapsid relatives took over the seas and skies.

Pseudosuchians had been displaced from their position atop terrestrial ecosystems, and all but two lineages went extinct in the Triassic–Jurassic extinction. One of these, the sphenosuchians, survived as agile terrestrial forms until the end of the Jurassic, while the other, the crocodyliformes, are still alive today. Crocodyliformes were much more diverse in the Jurassic and Cretaceous than they are today, and they radiated into a diverse array of niches, including marine predators and even terrestrial herbivores.

The marine thalattosuchians shared the seas with ichthyosaurs and plesiosaurs. Ichthyosaurs were successful at the beginning of the Jurassic and they became highly specialized for life in the ocean, developing streamlined bodies, large eyes, and even layers of blubber for insulation similar to modern whales and dolphins. Some of the carnivorous plesiosaurs became enormous in the middle of the Jurassic and they displaced ichthyosaurs as the top predators of the seas.

The flying pterosaurs became exceptionally diverse in the Jurassic and spread worldwide. Most Jurassic pterosaurs remained small and retained a mouthful of conical teeth for catching insects or fish. Toward the end of the Jurassic, the pterodactyloids arose. They lacked the long tail of earlier pterosaurs and were able to reach much larger sizes. Many lost their teeth later in the Cretaceous.

| Group: ICHTHYOPTERYGIA | Subgroup: Ichthyosauria | Time: 201–174 mya |

Temnodontosaurus

TEM-NOH-DON-TOH-SAW-RUS

This large ichthyosaur looked a bit like a modern dolphin. Its body was long, smooth, and streamlined, and it had a long, narrow snout, with many large teeth set into a dental groove. Its tail was large, and it had four long, narrow paddles. Unusually, the rear paddles were almost the same length as the front ones. *Temnodontosaurus* also had a large triangular dorsal fin, as did all advanced ichthyosaurs. Fossil finds of ichthyosaur young preserved inside the body of adults show that these creatures were viviparous—they gave birth to live young in the sea without having to come ashore to lay eggs.

DESCRIBED BY Lydekker 1889
HABITAT Shallow seas

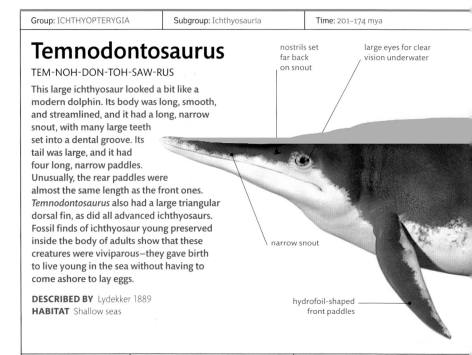

nostrils set far back on snout

large eyes for clear vision underwater

narrow snout

hydrofoil-shaped front paddles

| Length: 30 ft (9 m) | Weight: ~16½ tons (15 metric tons) | Diet: Large squid, ammonites |

Group: ICHTHYOPTERYGIA	Subgroup: Ichthyosauria	Time: 205–182 mya

Ichthyosaurus
IK-THEE-OH-SAW-RUS

Hundreds of complete skeletons of *Ichthyosaurus* have been discovered, making it one of the best-known of all prehistoric animals. It had a high dorsal fin and broad front paddles. The end section of the tail was angled downward to support the vertical tail fin. *Ichthyosaurus* had massive ear bones, possibly to pick up underwater vibrations created by potential prey.

DESCRIBED BY de la Beche and Conybeare 1821
HABITAT Oceans

smooth skin

half-moon-shaped tail fin

small, pointed teeth

very short rear paddles

Length: 11 ft (3.3 m)	Weight: ~200 lb (90 kg)	Diet: Fish

tapered body

large tail fin for propulsion

| Group: ICHTHYOPTERYGIA | Subgroup: Ichthyosauria | Time: 174–163 mya |

Ophthalmosaurus

OFF-THAL-MO-SAW-RUS

It is not difficult to see why *Ophthalmosaurus* ("eye lizard") was so named. Its eyes were the largest of any creature relative to body size. As in other ichthyosaurs, the eyes were surrounded by the sclerotic ring—a circular arrangement of bony plates that prevented the soft tissues from collapsing at high pressures. Some paleontologists think that *Ophthalmosaurus* had such large eyes because it was a night hunter that swam at very deep depths. *Ophthalmosaurus* had a teardrop-shaped body. The tail had a crescent-shaped fin. The paddles were short and broad.

DESCRIBED BY Seeley 1874
HABITAT Oceans

nostrils set high on snout, close to eyes

huge eye sockets

long, thin snout

| Length: 20 ft (6 m) | Weight: ~3½ tons (3 metric tons) | Diet: Fish, squid, other mollusks |

| Group: PLESIOSAURIA | Subgroup: Plesiosauroidea | Time: 199–190 mya |

Plesiosaurus

PLEEZ-EE-OH-SAW-RUS

Plesiosaurus was built for maneuverability rather than speed. It had the typical plesiosaur shape of a short and wide body that tapered toward the tail. Its neck was much longer than the body and was very flexible. Although its head was relatively small, its jaws were long and held many sharp, conical teeth. *Plesiosaurus* had four wide paddle-shaped flippers, which it is thought to have used in a figure-eight pattern of paddling.

DESCRIBED BY de la Beche and Conybeare 1821
HABITAT Oceans

paddlelike flippers

small head

flexible neck longer than body

| Length: 7½ ft (2.5 m) | Weight: ~200 lb (90 kg) | Diet: Fish, squidlike mollusks |

vertebrae
supported
dorsal fin

flat, broad
paddles

massive body
more rounded
at front

digits elongated by
additional bones

nflexible spine

weak tail
not used for
propulsion

network of belly
ribs (gastralia)

| Group: PLESIOSAURIA | Subgroup: Plesiosauroidea | Time: 174–164 mya |

Cryptoclidus
CRIP-TOH-CLY-DUS

Cryptoclidus was a plesiosaur with a moderately long neck made up of 30 vertebrae. Its small skull had a long snout, with the nostrils set far back. Its jaw contained many sharp, pointed teeth. These interlocked when the jaw was closed to make a fine trap for small fish or shrimplike prey. *Cryptoclidus* had a relatively short tail and four hydrofoil-shaped flippers. These are thought to have been used in a figure-eight motion to propel the animal along. The shoulders and hips became large plates that supported powerful muscles which helped propel the plesiosaur. *Cryptoclidus* is thought to have given birth to live young.

DESCRIBED BY Seeley 1892
HABITAT Shallow oceans

long, relatively inflexible neck

| Length: 13 ft (4 m) | Weight: ~9 tons (8 metric tons) | Diet: Fish, small marine animals |

| Group: PLESIOSAURIA | Subgroup: Pliosauroidea | Time: 166–152 mya |

Liopleurodon
LIE-OH-PLOOR-OH-DON

Liopleurodon was a massive marine carnivore. It had a whalelike appearance, with a large, heavy head; a short, thick neck; and a streamlined body. It is thought to have used its front and rear flippers in different swimming motions, with the front pair moving up and down and the rear ones used in a figure-eight motion. Its teeth were arranged in a rosette at the front of its mouth. It may have swum with its mouth open, allowing water to pass into its nostrils so that it could smell its prey.

streamlined body

large eyes

DESCRIBED BY Sauvage 1873
HABITAT Oceans

rosette of teeth at front of jaw

base of vertebra

airfoil-shaped front flippers

Fossil vertebra

| Length: 16–23 ft (5–7 m) | Weight: Not calculated | Diet: Large squid, ichthyosaurs |

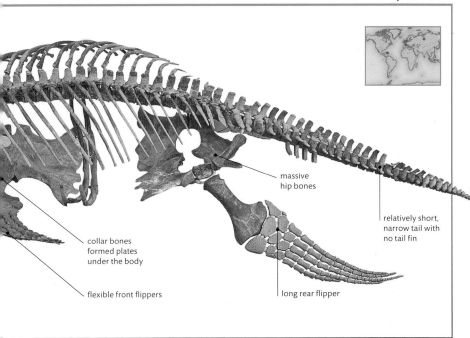

massive
hip bones

relatively short,
narrow tail with
no tail fin

collar bones
formed plates
under the body

flexible front flippers

long rear flipper

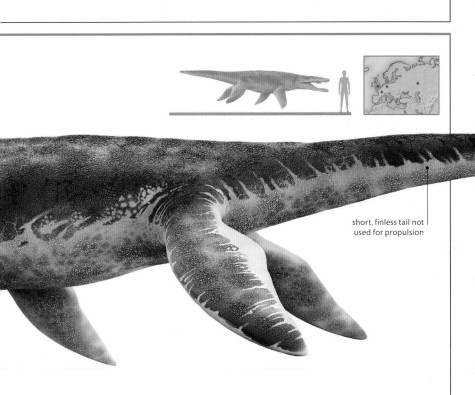

short, finless tail not
used for propulsion

Group: PSEUDOSUCHIA	Subgroup: Crocodyliformes	Time: 163–145 mya

Cricosaurus
CREE-COH-SAW-RUS

This "ring lizard" was a highly specialized aquatic crocodilian. It had a streamlined shape and had lost the heavy back armor that crocodiles normally have. Its smoother skin meant that *Cricosaurus* was more maneuverable when swimming and could move its body, as well as its tail, from side to side to propel itself along. It had two pairs of flippers and a large, fishlike tail fin, which was supported by a steep downward bend of the spine. One fossil specimen of *Cricosaurus* was found outlined by a thin film of carbon. This showed the shape of the limbs in life. The hind flippers were longer than the front pair, which were shaped like hydrofoils. The long, slim snout was filled with sharp, pointed teeth.

DESCRIBED BY Wagner 1858
HABITAT Seas

vertical tail fin

long, thin tail

hydrofoil-shaped front flippers

Length: 9¾ ft (3 m)	Weight: ~265 lb (120 kg)	Diet: Fish

Group: PSEUDOSUCHIA	Subgroup: Crocodyliformes	Time: 166–152 mya

Metriorhynchus
MET-REE-OR-RINE-CUS

An aquatic crocodilian, *Metriorhynchus* is now thought to have given birth to live young. It had a streamlined shape, although not as streamlined as its relative *Cricosaurus*, with a long, slim head; long body; and thin tail. Its skin was smooth, reducing resistance in the water, and it had a vertical, fishlike tail fin. Moving this from side to side propelled *Metriorhynchus* through the water. Its limbs were formed into paddles, with the hindlimbs being larger than the forelimbs. Its snout was long and pointed and the jaws had long muscles to allow the animal to open its mouth very wide. The teeth were conical.

DESCRIBED BY von Meyer 1832
HABITAT Tropical seas

long snout with nostrils set far forward

sharp, conical teeth

front paddles shorter than hind

Length: 9¾ ft (3 m)	Weight: ~265 lb (120 kg)	Diet: Fish

steep bend in spine to support tail fin

Fossil skeleton

hind flipper

short neck

long, slim snout

nostrils at tip of snout

sharp, pointed teeth

smooth skin

tail fin moved from side to side

flipper-shaped hindlimb

sharp downward bend in tail

well-developed joint surfaces for strength when bending

slim snout

Fossil skull

relatively large eye sockets

large attachment sites for jaw muscles

Fossil vertebra

Group: ARCHOSAURIA	Subgroup: Pterosauria	Time: 201–182 mya

Dimorphodon

DIE-MOR-FOH-DON

The most striking feature of *Dimorphodon* ("two-form tooth") was its enormous puffinlike head. It had a short neck and a long tail. The tail could only be moved near the base, helping steer the animal. It was probably a clumsy walker. *Dimorphodon* was a relatively poor flier that is suggested to have spent most of its time hanging from cliffs or branches. It is thought to have been a quadrupedal climbing animal that used its short wings for short flights only as a last resort. *Dimorphodon* had two types of teeth—long front ones and small cheek teeth.

DESCRIBED BY Owen 1859
HABITAT Shores

long front teeth

Length: 4 ft (1.4 m)	Weight: Not calculated	Diet: Fish

Group: ARCHOSAURIA	Subgroup: Pterosauria	Time: 150–148 mya

Rhamphorhynchus

RAM-FOR-RINK-US

This pterosaur is well-known from beautifully preserved specimens found along with *Archaeopteryx*. Details of the wing structure and the tail can be seen, and a throat pouch has even been preserved in a few fossils. *Rhamphorhynchus* had long, narrow jaws to act as a fish spear. Its sharp teeth pointed outward. It had a long tail, with a diamond-shaped flap of skin at the end, and small legs. The wing membrane stretched down to the ankle.

DESCRIBED BY von Meyer 1847
HABITAT Shores

large eyes

outward-pointing
teeth at end of jaws

Length: 3¼ ft (1 m)	Weight: ~44 lb (20 kg)	Diet: Fish

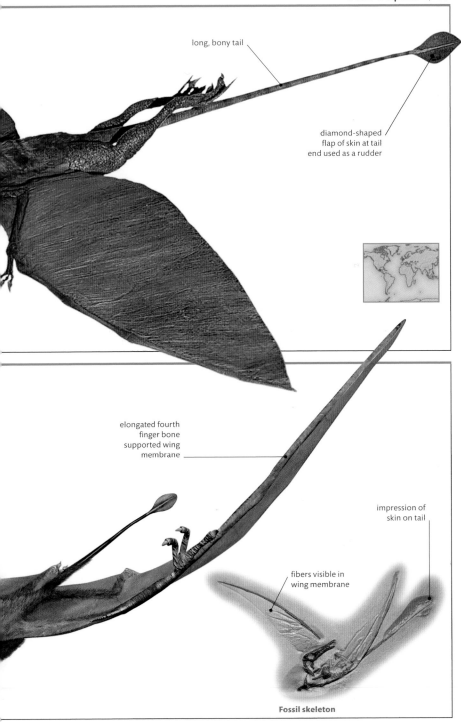

long, bony tail

diamond-shaped
flap of skin at tail
end used as a rudder

elongated fourth
finger bone
supported wing
membrane

impression of
skin on tail

fibers visible in
wing membrane

Fossil skeleton

Group: ARCHOSAURIA	Subgroup: Pterosauria	Time: 150–148 mya

Anurognathus

AN-YOOR-OG-NATH-US

This tiny pterosaur was unlike other rhamphorhynchoids in that it only had a very short tail. In fact, its name means "without tail and jaw." Along with the short tail, its small body size would have made maneuvering on wings very easy. *Anurognathus* is now known to have a very short, broad skull, similar to a modern nightjar. The peglike teeth were used for catching insects. Its wings, which reached a maximum span of about 20 in (50 cm), were composed of a thin flap of skin that stretched from the elongated fourth finger to the ankle. A secondary wing, supported by the pteroid bone, stretched from each wrist to the neck.

DESCRIBED BY Döderlein 1923
HABITAT Wooded plains

thin, delicate
wing membrane

Length: 3½ in (9 cm)	Weight: ~¼ oz (7 g)	Diet: Insects

Group: PTEROSAURIA	Subgroup: Pterodactyloidea	Time: 150–148 mya

Pterodactylus

TER-OH-DAK-TIL-US

Of the many species of *Pterodactylus* ("wing finger") originally discovered, most have now been grouped into a single species, while those that remain separate have been moved to other genera. Only one species of *Pterodactylus* is currently recognized. It had a long, curved, pelicanlike neck and a long skull with many small, pointed teeth. Skeletal analysis shows that it was a powerful, active flier.

DESCRIBED BY Cuvier 1809
HABITAT Shores

small,
lightweight
body

neck
outstretched
for flying

long, lightweight
arm bones

elongated fourth
digit supporting
wing membrane

Length: 3¼ ft (1 m)	Weight: ~2–11 lb (1–5 kg)	Diet: Fish

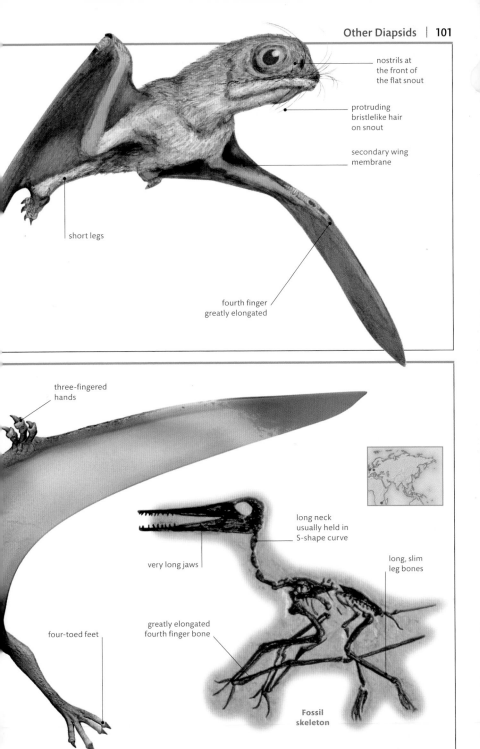

nostrils at the front of the flat snout

protruding bristlelike hair on snout

secondary wing membrane

short legs

fourth finger greatly elongated

three-fingered hands

long neck usually held in S-shape curve

very long jaws

long, slim leg bones

four-toed feet

greatly elongated fourth finger bone

Fossil skeleton

SYNAPSIDS

ONLY THE CYNODONTS survived into the Jurassic, and even then, only a select few lineages.

For a long time, we knew very little about these "proto-mammals," called Mammaliaformes, because their fossil record consists mostly of teeth and rare jaws. It was therefore believed that throughout the Jurassic and most of the Cretaceous, mammals and their close relatives were struggling to survive in the shadows of the dinosaurs.

In the last 25 years, this view has been radically changed by a trove of incredible fossils from the Jurassic found in China. These beds preserve some of the oldest true mammals, and they show that three lineages—docodonts, haramiyidans, and multituberculates—were incredibly

diverse. These groups include not only nocturnal insectivores, but swimmers, climbers, diggers, and even gliders.

These fossils also record the gradual accumulation of the features we now consider characteristic of mammals, including specialized teeth, with a complex topography of cusps, basins, and crests. To stabilize these new teeth for precise chewing motions, the tooth-bearing jawbone, called the dentary, became anchored to the skull, and the smaller jawbones behind it were reduced. These small bones were eventually incorporated into the hearing apparatus, part of a series of changes that heightened the senses of mammals. These adaptations allowed early mammals to acquire the energy needed to drive their fast metabolisms.

Group: MAMMALIAFORMES	Subgroup: Docodonta	Time: 156–149 mya

Docodon

DOH-CO-DON

Docodon ("beam tooth") was a mouse-sized, close mammal relative. So far, this genus is known only from remains of jaws and teeth. These had very complex tooth cusp patterns, allowing *Docodon* to chew food effectively. It appears to have been a rodentlike animal and was probably endothermic.

DESCRIBED BY
Marsh 1881
HABITAT
Forests

probably fur-covered body

five-toed feet

Length: 4 in (10 cm)	Weight: ~¾–1¾ oz (20–50 g)	Diet: Possibly omnivorous

Group: CYNODONTIA	Subgroup: Mammaliaformes	Time: 199–190 mya

Sinoconodon

SINE-OH-CO-DON

Sinoconodon ("Chinese spiky tooth") was a small, primitive mammal resembling a modern shrew. Its skull structure, despite retaining some early cynodont characters, showed that it was very closely related to true mammals. In particular, the structures housing the inner ear are similar to those of true mammals. Although the cheek teeth were permanent, as in living mammals, its other teeth were still replaced several times during its lifetime, like in earlier cynodonts. The rear of the braincase had expanded and the eye socket was large. *Sinoconodon* was apparently endothermic and was probably covered in fur. It was a quadruped, with five long, clawed toes on each foot and a long tail. The snout was long and slim.

DESCRIBED BY Patterson and Olson 1961
HABITAT Woodland

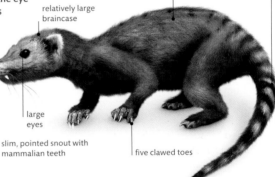

fur-covered body

long, flexible tail

relatively large braincase

large eyes

slim, pointed snout with mammalian teeth

five clawed toes

Length: 4–6 in (10–15 cm)	Weight: ~1–2⅞ oz (30–80 g)	Diet: Probably mainly insects

Group: MAMMALIAFORMES	Subgroup: Mammalia	Time: 152–139 mya

Triconodon

TRY-CON-OH-DON

Triconodon ("three-spiked tooth") was a small raccoon- or possumlike early mammal. Originally classed in the same group as *Eozostrodon* (see p.57), recent analysis shows that it was a true mammal. Its teeth were rather unspecialized and versatile, suggesting an omnivorous lifestyle, including insects and small reptiles. The development of a mammalian middle ear seems to have coincided with an increase in brain size.

DESCRIBED BY Owen 1859
HABITAT Woodland

molars with three sharp points

large teeth at the front of the jaw

Fossil jawbone

Length: 20 in (50 cm)	Weight: ~1¾ lb (750 g)	Diet: Omnivorous

CRETACEOUS PERIOD

145–66 MILLION YEARS AGO

THE CLIMATE in the Cretaceous was similar to that in the Jurassic—warm and humid. Sea levels were very high, resulting in large areas of flooding and consequent isolation of landmasses. A major evolutionary development—the diversification of the angiosperms (flowering plants)—led to important changes in the landscape and animal life on Earth. Many new insect groups appeared, and dinosaurs continued to flourish. Populations of certain groups, such as sauropods and stegosaurs, were greatly reduced, as their staple food supply was taken over by new dinosaur groups, including the advanced ornithopods and ceratopsians. These flourished until the mass extinction event at the end of the period.

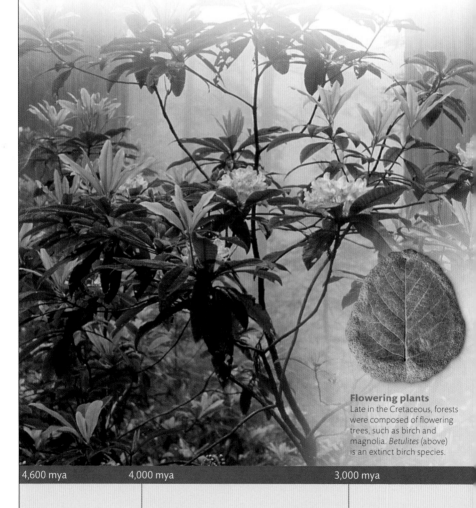

Flowering plants
Late in the Cretaceous, forests were composed of flowering trees, such as birch and magnolia. *Betulites* (above) is an extinct birch species.

4,600 mya   4,000 mya   3,000 mya

CRETACEOUS LANDMASSES

During the Cretaceous, continental drift led to the break-up of the supercontinents of Laurasia and Gondwana. This process was augmented by the very high sea levels of 640 ft (200 m). The Atlantic Ocean started to open up between the future South America and Africa, and Antarctica was almost in its modern position. India started to move northward. There was still a land link between Eurasia and North America.

CRETACEOUS LIFE

Dinosaurs were still the dominant land animals. They increased in diversity throughout the period, with new groups such as the hadrosaurs, horned dinosaurs, and giant tyrannosaurs appearing. Birds continued to evolve, and snakes appeared. Mammals were still small but continued to diversify.

Mammal evolution
Mammals remained only minor elements of the fauna. Like the early marsupial *Didelphodon*, (right) they were shrew- or cat-sized animals.

webbed toes

neck frill with
large openings

Ceratopsians
The Cretaceous saw the appearance of the frilled ceratopsian dinosaurs, such as *Chasmosaurus* (left). These had brow and nose horns and a large, bony frill covering the neck and shoulders.

wide feet

2,000 mya   1,000 mya   500 mya   250 mya   0

THEROPODS

THEROPODS REACHED their peak in diversity in the Cretaceous. Ceratosaurs and carnosaurs remained the top predators in the Early Cretaceous, and some, such as *Giganotosaurus* and *Spinosaurus*, reached enormous sizes in the early parts of the Late Cretaceous.

During the mid-Cretaceous, ecosystems underwent drastic changes alongside the spread of flowering plants. Some coelurosaurian theropods became larger and started to displace the ruling tetanuran theropods. In Laurasia, the ceratosaurs and carnosaurs became extinct, possibly because of the decline of certain sauropods, but in Gondwana, these groups persisted with coelurosaurs until the end of the Cretaceous. Tyrannosaurids

filled the void of Late Cretaceous apex predators in Laurasia, spreading throughout Asia and North America.

Some coelurosaur groups, such as the sickle-clawed dromaeosaurs and troodontids, became highly specialized. Others, such as therizinosaurs, oviraptorosaurs, and ornithomimosaurs, became herbivorous, losing teeth and developing a keratinous beak instead.

During the Early Cretaceous, toothed enantiornithine birds were common, but toothless ornithurine birds became predominant by Late Cretaceous. It was debated whether modern bird lineages arose before or after the extinction, but new fossils now conclusively show that they originated in the latest Cretaceous.

Group: CERATOSAURIA	Subgroup: Abelisauridae	Time: 83–78 mya

Abelisaurus

AH-BEL-EE-SAW-RUS

relatively small teeth

This large theropod, named for its discoverer, Roberto Abel, is known only from a single skull. It seems to have been a rather primitive form related to *Carnotaurus*. Its head was large, with a rounded snout, and its teeth were relatively small for a carnivorous dinosaur of its size. Its skull is peculiar in that it has a huge opening at the side just above the jaws, which is much larger than in other dinosaurs. Reconstructions of the rest of its body are necessarily hypothetical. The illustration here is based on the body structure of *Carnotaurus* and similar theropod dinosaurs.

DESCRIBED BY Bonaparte 1984
HABITAT River plains

probably three-fingered hands

typical body shape of large theropods

bipedal stance

probably three-clawed toes

Length: 30 ft (9 m)	Weight: ~1⅜ tons (1.4 metric tons)	Diet: Meat

Group: CERATOSAURIA	Subgroup: Abelisauridae	Time: 82–66 mya

Carnotaurus

KAR-NOH-TAW-RUS

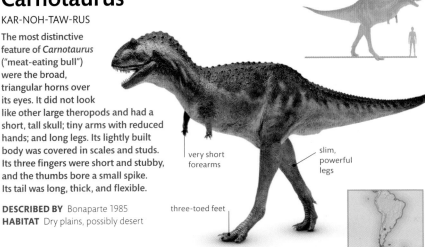

The most distinctive feature of *Carnotaurus* ("meat-eating bull") were the broad, triangular horns over its eyes. It did not look like other large theropods and had a short, tall skull; tiny arms with reduced hands; and long legs. Its lightly built body was covered in scales and studs. Its three fingers were short and stubby, and the thumbs bore a small spike. Its tail was long, thick, and flexible.

very short forearms

slim, powerful legs

three-toed feet

DESCRIBED BY Bonaparte 1985
HABITAT Dry plains, possibly desert

Length: 25 ft (7.5 m)	Weight: ~1 ton (1 metric ton)	Diet: Meat

Group: CARNOSAURIA	Subgroup: Carcharodontosauridae	Time: 100–96 mya

Giganotosaurus

GIG-AN-OH-TOE-SAW-RUS

large eyes

Giganotosaurus ("giant southern lizard") is one of the largest carnivorous dinosaurs yet discovered. Its skull was longer than an average man and held long, serrated teeth. Its hands had three fingers and it had a slim, pointed tail. Although larger than *Tyrannosaurus*, it was more lightly built than that dinosaur and seems to have hunted in a different fashion—by slashing at its prey rather than charging and biting head on. Despite its huge size, some paleontologists maintain that, like other large theropods, it may have been able to run relatively fast.

serrated teeth 8 in (20 cm) long

DESCRIBED BY Coria and Salgado 1995
HABITAT Warm swamps

three clawed fingers

Length: 41 ft (12.5 m)	Weight: ~7⅞ tons (8 metric tons)	Diet: Meat

| Group: CARNOSAURIA | Subgroup: Spinosauridae | Time: 98–94 mya |

Spinosaurus

SPINE-OH-SAW-RUS

Spinosaurus ("spine lizard") was an immense theropod with a crocodilelike snout and a sail running all the way down its back. It was among the largest carnivores to ever walk the Earth, rivaling *Giganotosaurus* and *Tyrannosaurus* in size, but its exact length remains uncertain. New discoveries show that the hindlimbs were short and the tail was tall and paddlelike, which may have been adapted to suit a semiaquatic lifestyle. However, a number of paleontologists have argued that some of the fossils are from a different, closely related spinosaur and that the sail on its back would have made it unstable while swimming.

DESCRIBED BY Stromer 1915
HABITAT Tropical swamps

tooth socket

Fossil tooth battery

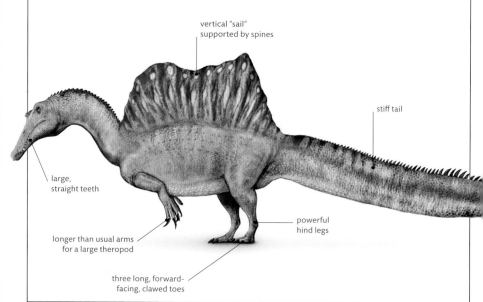

vertical "sail"
supported by spines

stiff tail

large,
straight teeth

longer than usual arms
for a large theropod

three long, forward-
facing, clawed toes

powerful
hind legs

| Length: 49–59 ft (15–18 m) | Weight: ~7 tons (7.1 metric tons) | Diet: Meat, possibly fish |

Group: CARNOSAURIA	Subgroup: Spinosauridae	Time: 129–125 mya

Suchomimus

SOOK-OH-MIME-US

This dinosaur, whose name means "crocodile mimic," had several features that indicate that it ate fish. It had a very long snout and huge, curved thumb claws that could be used for hooking fish from the water. The jaws had over 100 teeth that pointed slightly backward, and the end of the snout had a rosette of longer teeth. A low ridge ran along the length of its back. Its arms were relatively long, which would have enabled *Suchomimus* to reach into the water to grasp prey.

DESCRIBED BY Sereno et al. 1998
HABITAT Lush forests

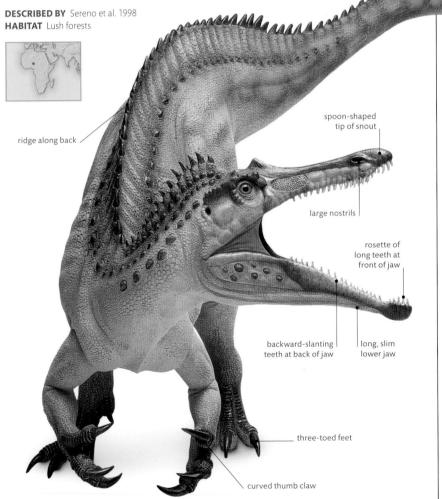

ridge along back

spoon-shaped
tip of snout

large nostrils

rosette of
long teeth at
front of jaw

backward-slanting
teeth at back of jaw

long, slim
lower jaw

three-toed feet

curved thumb claw

Length: 36 ft (11 m)	Weight: ~5 tons (5.1 metric tons)	Diet: Fish, possibly meat

Group: CARNOSAURIA	Subgroup: Spinosauridae	Time: 129–125 mya

Baryonyx

BAR-EE-ON-ICKS

Baryonyx ("heavy claw") was named for one of its unusual features—
its huge, curved thumb claws. Its skull was also an unusual shape for
a theropod, being long and narrow, similar to that of a crocodile.
There was a bony crest on the top of the head, and the jaws were filled
with 96 pointed and serrated teeth. This is twice as many as theropods
usually possessed. Its arms were thick and unusually powerful. These
features, along with the remains of fish found with the skeleton, have
led paleontologists to surmise that *Baryonyx* fished using its claws as
hooks, in the same way that a modern bear does.

DESCRIBED BY Charig and Milner 1986
HABITAT Riverbanks

bony head crest

curved neck

BARYONYX CLAW

Although the thumb claws were not found
attached to the skeleton, they were initially
suspected to have been from the foot. However,
recent finds have now made it clear that they
formed part of the hand. Paleontologists
reconstructed *Baryonyx* with the claws in this
position because the length and thickness of
the arms seemed to match their proportions.

sharp, curved
thumb claw
12 in (30 cm) long

unusually
thick, powerful
arm bones

sharp claws on
other fingers

Length: 33 ft (10 m)	Weight: ~2 tons (2 metric tons)	Diet: Fish, perhaps meat

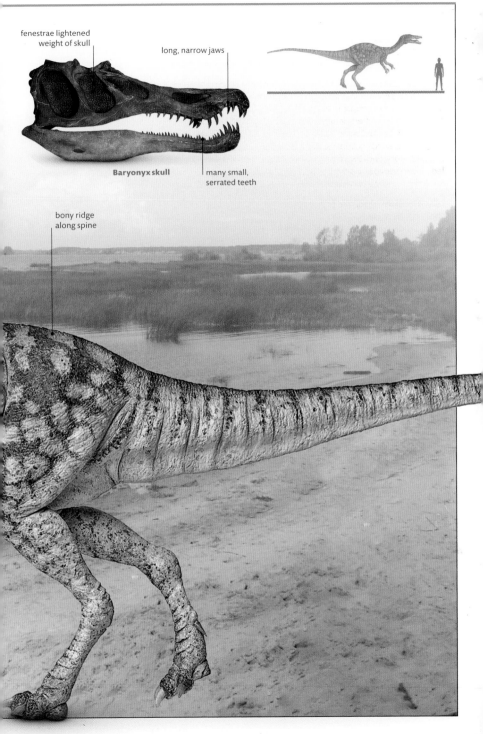

fenestrae lightened
weight of skull

long, narrow jaws

Baryonyx skull

many small,
serrated teeth

bony ridge
along spine

Group: COELUROSAURIA	Subgroup: Tyrannosauridae	Time: 68–66 mya

Tyrannosaurus
TIE-RAN-OH-SAW-RUS

Tyrannosaurus ("tyrant lizard") was one of the largest terrestrial carnivores ever. It was a heavily built theropod, with thick, long, powerful legs and a large, deep head. Paleontologists debated whether it was an active predator or simply a scavenger and how fast it actually was. However, recent analysis shows that *Tyrannosaurus* was a predator that would opportunistically scavenge. Evidence supporting this includes numerous healed bites from tyrannosaurs found on hadrosaur and ceratopsian bones, showing that it was hunting them while they were alive. For most of its lifetime, *Tyrannosaurus* would have been able to run as quickly as its prey, but eventually it was restricted to a walking gait due to its body size. The presence of feathers on its body is still debated, but skin impressions show that most of the animal was covered in pebbly scales. If feathers were present, they were limited to the back.

DESCRIBED BY Osborn 1905
HABITAT Open forests, coastal forested swamps

pebbled skin texture

6-in (15-cm) long, serrated teeth

New discovery
In 1990, a new specimen of *Tyrannosaurus* was discovered in South Dakota. The skeleton is named Sue, after its discoverer Sue Hendrickson, and is 90 percent complete.

Length: 40 ft (12 m)	Weight: ~6⅝ tons (6.7 metric tons)		Diet: Hadrosaurs, ceratopsians

TYRANNOSAURUS SKELETON

The first skeletal reconstruction of *Tyrannosaurus* was prepared in 1915, showing the dinosaur standing upright with its tail along the ground. Recent analysis has shown that the backbone was held horizontally, with the body perfectly balanced at the hips.

large fenestrae to lighten skull

12 back vertebrae with holes to reduce weight

tail made up of about 40 vertebrae

58 teeth

relatively slim, birdlike foot

saurischian hip

tail held stiffly for balance

tail heavily muscled at base

long, heavily muscled legs

Group: COELUROSAURIA	Subgroup: Tyrannosauridae	Time: 72–68 mya

Alioramus

AL-EE-OH-RAY-MUS

Alioramus ("different branch") was a small relative of *Tyrannosaurus rex* with a long, slender snout. Adorning the snout and skull were multiple small horns and bumps that may have been used in mating displays. The lighter build of *Alioramus* compared to its larger cousins likely reflected their different prey preferences. *Alioramus* probably ate small animals instead of bigger ceratopsians and hadrosaurs.

elongated snout with small horns and bumps

short arms, like other tyrannosaurs

long, agile legs

DESCRIBED BY Kurzanov 1976
HABITAT Woodland

Length: 16 ft (5 m)	Weight: ~813½ lb (369 kg)	Diet: Meat

Group: COELUROSAURIA	Subgroup: Compsognathidae	Time: 124–122 mya

Sinosauropteryx

SIEN-OH-SORE-OP-TUH-RIKS

Sinosauropteryx ("Chinese lizard wing") was the first dinosaur discovered with feather impressions. These feathers were simpler than those of living birds; they looked more like filaments. By studying the pigment-holding structures of these feathers, paleontologists have learned that *Sinosauropteryx* was reddish-brown, with a striped tail. Its countershaded body would have allowed it to camouflage effectively in the open environments it inhabited.

fuzzy feathers

striped tail for camouflage

relatively short arms

DESCRIBED BY
Ji and Ji 1996
HABITAT
Open forests

three clawed toes

Length: 3 ft (1 m)	Weight: ~18 oz (500 g)	Diet: Lizards, small animals

Group: COELUROSAURIA	Subgroup: Ornithomimidae	Time: 72–68 mya

Gallimimus

GAL-EE-MY-MUS

Gallimimus ("chicken mimic") is one of the best-known of the ornithomimids, or "bird mimic" dinosaurs. It had a short body with a long, stiff tail and slim legs built for running at high speed. Its neck was slender and flexible, and the skull ended in a long, toothless beak. The braincase was relatively large, and *Gallimimus* was probably quite intelligent. Its eyes were large, but it did not have stereoscopic vision.

DESCRIBED BY Osmólska et al. 1972
HABITAT Desert plains

large eye socket

toothless beak

Fossil skull

slender feet with three toes

long, grasping arms

Length: 20 ft (6 m)	Weight: ~880 lb (400 kg)	Diet: Omnivorous

Group: COELUROSAURIA	Subgroup: Ornithomimosauria	Time: 72–68 mya

Deinocheirus

DINE-OH-KIRE-US

The first remains of *Deinocheirus* were an enormous pair of arms 8 ft (2.4 m) long, which gave rise to the dinosaur's name—"terrible hand." New specimens show that *Deinocheirus* was one of the ornithomimosaurs, or "bird mimic" dinosaurs. It had a long, low skull with a deep lower jaw and a duck beak. There was a hump on its back above its hips, its hindlimbs were short, and its feet were broad with hooflike claws. Gastroliths and fish remains were preserved in its stomach, which suggests that it was an omnivore.

body and tail probably similar to other theropods

DESCRIBED BY Kielan-Jaworowska 1969
HABITAT Desert

three fingers on each hand

10-in (25-cm) long claws

Length: 36 ft (11 m)	Weight: ~6.9 tons (6,300 kg)	Diet: Omnivore

Group: COELUROSAURIA	Subgroup: Ornithomimidae	Time: 77–76 mya

Struthiomimus

STRUTH-EE-OH-MY-MUS

For many years after its first discovery, *Struthiomimus* ("ostrich mimic") was thought to be the same dinosaur as *Ornithomimus* (below). The two dinosaurs are remarkably similar—the main difference is that *Struthiomimus* had longer arms with stronger fingers. In addition, its thumbs did not oppose the fingers. This reduced the grasping ability of the hands. *Struthiomimus*, like all of the other "bird mimics," had a small head with a toothless beak and a long, stiff tail.

DESCRIBED BY Osborn 1917
HABITAT Open country, riverbanks

small head

strong fingers

long foot bones

Length: 11 ft (3.5 m)	Weight: ~330 lb (150 kg)	Diet: Omnivorous

Group: COELUROSAURIA	Subgroup: Ornithomimidae	Time: 77–67 mya

Ornithomimus

OR-NITH-OH-MY-MUS

This "bird mimic" is typical of its family. It had slim arms and long, slim legs. Its tail made up more than half of its length and was kept stiff by a network of ligaments. Its small head had a toothless beak and was held upright by an S-shaped bend in the long, flexible neck. The brain cavity was relatively large. *Ornithomimus* ran with its body held horizontally and its tail outstretched for balance. Its top speed has been estimated at up to 30 mph (50 kph).

impression of toes

Fossil footprints

DESCRIBED BY
Marsh 1890
HABITAT
Swamps, forests

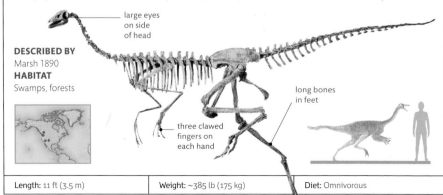

large eyes on side of head

long bones in feet

three clawed fingers on each hand

Length: 11 ft (3.5 m)	Weight: ~385 lb (175 kg)	Diet: Omnivorous

Group: COELUROSAURIA	Subgroup: Alvarezsauridae	Time: 83–76 mya

Shuvuuia

SHU-VOO-EE-A

Since its discovery, *Shuvuuia* (its name is derived from "*shuvuu*," the Mongolian word for bird) has provoked great debate as to whether it was a dinosaurlike bird or a birdlike dinosaur. It is now clear that *Shuvuuia* and its kin were not birds, but they had converged on some of the distinctive features of modern birds. Although *Shuvuuia* did not have a true beak, its slender jaws bore tiny teeth, and it may have been able to raise its upper jaw in relation to the braincase, a facility only modern birds have. Chemical analysis also shows that it was feathered. The legs were long and slim, suggesting that it may have been a fast runner. The forelimbs were short and stubby and ended in a single, clawed digit. These unusual arms were probably used for digging at insect nests.

DESCRIBED BY Chiappe et al. 1998
HABITAT Woodland

head very like that of modern birds

long, slender neck

claw on digit may have been used for opening termite nests

long, slim legs

feet with three forward-facing, clawed toes

Length: 2 ft (1 m)	Weight: ~5½ lb (2.5 kg)	Diet: Insects, small reptiles

Group: COELUROSAURIA	Subgroup: Therizinosauridae	Time: 72–68 mya

Therizinosaurus

THER-IZ-IN-OH-SAW-RUS

One of the strangest dinosaurs, the reconstruction of *Therizinosaurus* ("scythe lizard") is based on finds of other members of the family. Little is known of it apart from its incredibly long arms. These had three fingers that ended in curved, flat-sided claws, the first of which was longer than a person's arm. The claws seem too blunt for use in attack. Suggestions for their function have included that they were used in courtship or for raking plants. *Therizinosaurus* seems to have been an independent group, unrelated to *Oviraptors* as it had been suggested before.

claws up to 24 in (60 cm) long

Fossil scythe claw

toothless beak

fine, hairy feathers may have covered the skin

three clawed fingers

DESCRIBED BY
Maleev 1954
HABITAT
Woodland

Length: 36 ft (11 m)	Weight: Not calculated	Diet: Meat or possibly plants

Group: COELUROSAURIA	Subgroup: Oviraptorosauria	Time: 76–68 mya

Citipati

CHIT-I-PUH-TIH

Citipati is one of the oviraptorid dinosaurs, which got their name ("egg thief") because the first specimen was discovered on a nest of eggs, thought to be those of *Protoceratops*. However, dozens of new specimens (see right) show that these were actually oviraptorid eggs and that oviraptorids brooded their nests just like chickens. Like most oviraptorids, *Citipati* had an unusual, short head with a tall crest and a beak, which would have allowed them to have an omnivorous diet of plants and small prey. Fossils of its close relatives show that *Citipati* and other oviraptorosaurs were feathered.

hornlike crest on snout

clutch of eggs

Fossilized nest site

short beak

DESCRIBED BY
Clark et al. 2001
HABITAT Semidesert

bird-like feet

Length: 8 ft (2.5 m)	Weight: ~231 lb (105 kg)	Diet: Plants, small prey

Group: COELUROSAURIA	Subgroup: Oviraptorosauria	Time: 130–122 mya

Caudipteryx

CAWD-EE-TER-IKS

The discovery of this small, feathered dinosaur provided firm evidence of a theropod ancestry for birds. *Caudipteryx* ("tail feather") was a theropod with feathers covering its arms, most of its body, and its short tail. The feathers varied in structure—some were downy and others were structured quills with shafts and veins. The feathers were symmetrical, showing that this animal did not fly. It is now thought that complex feathers of this kind evolved in an earlier, flightless theropod and were inherited by both *Caudipteryx* and the ancestor of modern birds.

DESCRIBED BY Ji et al. 1998
HABITAT Lakesides

pointed beak with cluster of teeth at front of upper jaw

small, short skull with no teeth in lower jaw

short arms with symmetrical feathers

long, slim legs best-suited to running

birdlike feet with three forward-facing clawed toes

Length: 35 in (90 cm)	Weight: ~22 lb (10 kg)	Diet: Plants

| Group: PARAVES | Subgroup: Dromaeosauridae | Time: 120 mya |

Microraptor

MIKE-ROW-RAP-TOR

In addition to wings on the forelimbs, *Microraptor* ("tiny thief") also had wings on its hindlimbs. The microstructure of these feathers shows that it was an iridescent black color, similar to modern starlings. While it was initially thought that *Microraptor* could only use its four wings for gliding, recent studies have shown it was probably capable of powered flight. It may have used short bursts of flight to capture lizards and fish, which have been found in its stomach contents.

DESCRIBED BY Xu et al. 2000
HABITAT Forests and lakes

wings with complex, branching feathers

wings of feathers on the legs, as well as the arms

iridescent black plumage

diamond-shaped feather fan for stability

| Length: 3 ft (1 m) | Weight: ~12¼ oz (350 g) | Diet: Lizards, fish |

| Group: PARAVES | Subgroup: Dromaeosauridae | Time: 108–98 mya |

Deinonychus

DIE-NO-NIKE-US

One of the most fearsome predators of the Cretaceous, *Deinonychus* ("terrible claw") was named for the sickle-shaped claws on the second toe of each foot. New research shows that these were most effective as puncture weapons. *Deinonychus* may have leapt onto and restrained prey with its sharp claws while it began to eat the animal alive. Although previously thought to be a pack hunter based on a group found alongside a large *Tenontosaurus* (see p.209), it is now believed that *Deinonychus* died in a predator trap, attracted by the carcass of *Tenontosaurus*.

DESCRIBED BY Ostrom 1969
HABITAT Forests

lightweight body

long hind legs

sickle-shaped claw held off ground while running

tail held rigid

| Length: 9¾–13 ft (3–4 m) | Weight: ~155 lb (70 kg) | Diet: Herbivorous dinosaurs |

| Group: PARAVES | Subgroup: Dromaeosauridae | Time: 77–76 mya |

Dromaeosaurus

DROM-AY-OH-SAW-RUS

Dromaeosaurus ("running lizard") was the first sickle-clawed dinosaur to be discovered. However, the difficulty in reconstructing it from the few bones found meant that its true classification was only realized after *Deinonychus* was described. This dinosaur was smaller than *Deinonychus* but otherwise very similar. Its body was slender, with long limbs and a large head. Its sharp claws would have been effective for restraining and piercing prey.

DESCRIBED BY Matthew and Brown 1922
HABITAT Forests, plains

birdlike hip bones

large eye socket

sharp, backward-facing teeth

large braincase indicating relatively high intelligence

| Length: 5½ ft (1.8 m) | Weight: ~33 lb (15 kg) | Diet: Herbivorous dinosaurs |

Group: PARAVES	Subgroup: Dromaeosauridae	Time: 83–76 mya

Velociraptor

VEL-O-SEE-RAP-TOR

Many well-preserved skeletons of *Velociraptor* ("fast thief") have been found, making it the best-known member of its family. The main feature that sets it apart from other members of the family is its low, long, flat-snouted head. *Velociraptor* must have been a formidable predator—its jaws held about 80 very sharp teeth, and the second toe of each foot ended in a puncturing, sickle-shaped claw. The neck was S-shaped, and the hands bore three clawed fingers. It is probable that *Velociraptor* was a solitary predator. Traditionally reconstructed with scaly skin, recent analysis has shown that this dinosaur was covered in a downy coat or primitive feathers. It could not fly, but it would have had a wing with feathers, much like modern birds.

DESCRIBED BY Osborn 1924
HABITAT Woodland

Preserved in death
One of the most famous fossil finds is a *Velociraptor* and *Protoceratops* locked together in battle at the time of their deaths.

large eye socket

Fossil skull

long, slim jaws with pointed, recurved teeth

stiff tail held outstretched for balance

downy covering over much of body

slim legs with long shins for speed

large, sickle-shaped second claw

three-fingered grasping hands with claws

Length: 6 ft (1.8 m)	Weight: ~33 lb (15 kg)	Diet: Lizards, mammals, smaller dinosaurs

| Group: PARAVES | Subgroup: Troodontidae | Time: 83–76 mya |

Saurornithoides

SAWR-OR-NITH-OID-EEZ

Only the skull, a few arm bones, and teeth of *Saurornithoides* ("lizard bird form") have been found to date, but its classification as a troodontid is now certain. Its long, narrow skull had a relatively large braincase. Its long, powerful arms ended in three-fingered hands capable of grasping prey.

relatively large braincase

long, narrow snout

DESCRIBED BY
Osborn 1924
HABITAT Plains

jaw containing many sharp teeth

| Length: 6½–11 ft (2–3.5 m) | Weight: ~29–60 lb (13–27 kg) | Diet: Meat |

| Group: PARAVES | Subgroup: Troodontidae | Time: 83–76 mya |

Troodon

TROH-OH-DON

Troodon ("wounding tooth") was named for its sharp, serrated teeth. Its remains are very rare, and no complete skeleton has been found to date. Its reconstruction is based on the fossils found and details known from similar, closely related dinosaurs. It was probably an efficient hunter. It had long, slim hind legs; a large, sickle-shaped claw on both second toes; and three long, clawed fingers that were capable of grasping prey. The sickle claws were smaller than in *Deinonychus* (see p.121) and *Velociraptor* (opposite). This has led some paleontologists to suggest that they were mainly used for defense. *Troodon* could undoubtedly run quickly on its long legs, with its stiff tail held out behind for balance. Analysis of the slim skull shows that it had keen eyesight and may have had good hearing. Its braincase was also very large in proportion to its body size, indicating an unusually high level of intelligence for a dinosaur. *Troodon* eggs have been found in fossil nests.

large, keen eyes

slim, lightly built body

DESCRIBED BY Leidy 1856
HABITAT Plains

three-fingered hands

sickle-shaped claws on second toes

| Length: 6½ ft (2 m) | Weight: ~110 lb (50 kg) | Diet: Meat, carrion |

Group: PARAVES	Subgroup: Avialae	Time: 129–122 mya

Confuciusornis

CON-FUSH-EE-US-OAR-NIS

Confuciusornis ("Confucius bird") was the first bird known to have a true, horny beak. It had a mixture of primitive features (clawed wing fingers and a flat breastbone) and modern adaptations, such as a deeper chest and shortened tail core. The foot claws were highly curved, and the large toe was reversed, indicating that it was a tree dweller. Males had long tail feathers. Its beak turned up slightly at the end, leading to debate about its diet. *Confuciusornis* was most likely a side-shoot from the modern bird lineage.

DESCRIBED BY Hou et al. 1995
HABITAT Woodland

three wing fingers with curved claws

toothless, horny beak with slight upward curve

Length: 1 ft (31 cm)	Weight: Not calculated	Diet: Seeds, possibly fish

Group: AVIALAE	Subgroup: Ornithurae	Time: 84–78 mya

Hesperornis

HESS-PER-OAR-NISS

This large, toothed seabird lived a lifestyle very similar to that of modern penguins. It had lost the power of flight, and its vestigial wings were tiny and stubby. The head was long and low, with a long beak armed with sharp, pointed teeth for catching fish and other small marine creatures. *Hesperornis* ("western bird") was probably a powerful swimmer, using its large, webbed feet for propulsion, but may have moved clumsily on land. It probably nested on seashores.

DESCRIBED BY Marsh 1872
HABITAT Seashores

legs set far back

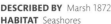

Length: 6½ ft (2 m)	Weight: Not calculated	Diet: Fish, squid

Group: AVIALAE	Subgroup: Ornithurae	Time: 95–83 mya

Ichthyornis

IK-THEE-OAR-NISS

When the jaw of this toothed, primitive bird was reexamined in 1952, it was thought for a time, incorrectly, to belong to a juvenile mosasaur. The jaws and teeth of *Ichthyornis* ("fish bird") are indeed similar to those of a marine reptile. *Ichthyornis* was a seabird, similar in size and build to a modern seagull, but its head and beak were much larger. It had a well-developed, keeled breastbone and a deep chest, suggesting it may have been a strong flier. Its webbed feet had claws.

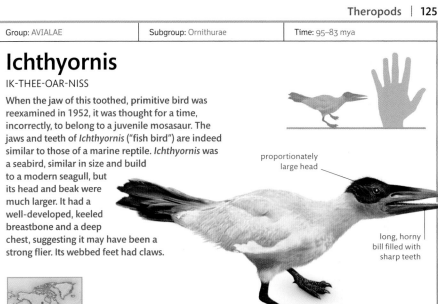

proportionately large head

long, horny bill filled with sharp teeth

webbed feet with short claws

DESCRIBED BY Marsh 1872
HABITAT Seashores

Length: 8 in (20 cm)	Weight: Not calculated	Diet: Fish

long neck that could be held in S-shape over shoulders

splintlike bones supported tiny wings

long, pointed, toothed beak

SAUROPODS

THE CRETACEOUS was the time of giants. It witnessed the rise of the appropriately named titanosaurs, which include the largest animals to ever walk on land. There is debate about which of the titanosaurs was the biggest, or even which measure is most important, but it is clear that *Argentinosaurus* from the Late Cretaceous was among them.

Titanosaurs became globally widespread, and have been found on every continent including Antarctica, but they were most common in the southern hemisphere. Communal nesting grounds show that they probably moved together in herds, and analyses of the internal structure of their bones suggest that they grew at exceptionally high rates to achieve their large sizes.

Titanosaurs persisted until the end of the Cretaceous, when they went extinct with the rest of the nonavian dinosaurs.

In contrast, diplodocoids and brachiosaurids only survived partway throughout the Cretaceous, and neither group made it to the end-Cretaceous extinction. Even though both of these groups were globally distributed in the Jurassic, their Early Cretaceous records are greatly restricted. Early Cretaceous brachiosaurids are known only from the southern part of North America and northwestern Gondwana, while diplodocoids were restricted to South America, Africa, and Europe. It is unclear why these groups declined and went extinct, but it was part of a broader restructuring of ecosystems across the Jurassic–Cretaceous boundary.

Group: SAUROPODA	Subgroup: Titanosauria	Time: 70–68 mya

Saltasaurus

SALT-AH-SAW-RUS

Saltasaurus was named for the province in Argentina where it was first found and was the first sauropod for which evidence of armor was found. The fossil remains consisted of a group of partial skeletons surrounded by thousands of bony plates. Most of these plates were tiny, but others were larger and may have ended in bony spikes. It is likely that these bony plates covered the back and sides of the dinosaur to form a protective covering. *Saltasaurus* had a long neck and a long, flexible tail. Its head was small, with a high skull. Like most sauropods, it would probably not have been able to rear up on its hind legs.

DESCRIBED BY Bonaparte and Powell 1980
HABITAT Woodland

long, flexible tail

Length: 39 ft (12 m)	Weight: ~19⅝ tons (20 metric tons)	Diet: Plants

Group: SAUROPODA	Subgroup: Titanosauria	Time: 93–89 mya

Argentinosaurus

AR-GEN-TEEN-OH-SAW-RUS

Only a few bones of *Argentinosaurus* (Argentina lizard) have been found to date, including some enormous vertebrae from the back, which were over 5 ft (1.5 m) wide in cross-section. Other bones found were the sacrum, a fibula, and a few ribs. Because of the sparsity of fossil evidence, very little is known about *Argentinosaurus*. However, it appears to have been the heaviest dinosaur ever known. As in other titanosaurs, the neck and tail would have been very long and thin, and the skull is likely to have been small and triangular.

DESCRIBED BY Bonaparte and Coria 1993
HABITAT Forested areas

long, slim neck

body thought to resemble that of other titanosaurs

long tail

elephantlike, thick limbs with clawed toes

Length: 98 ft (30 m)	Weight: ~106 tons (96 metric tons)	Diet: Conifers

bony plates and studs covering back and sides

nostrils high on head

neck shorter than tail

fossilized impressions of bony plates of varying sizes

Fossil armor

ORNITHISCHIANS

ALL MAJOR lineages of ornithischians survived into the Cretaceous and continued to thrive until the end-Cretaceous extinction.

While thyreophorans were larger and more successful in the Jurassic, cerapodans (the group including marginocephalians and ornithopods) took over in the Cretaceous. Ankylosaurs survived until the end of the period, but stegosaurs went extinct in the Early Cretaceous.

Iguanodontians, with distinctive thumb spikes, evolved from small bipedal ornithopods in the Early Cretaceous. In the Late Cretaceous, they gave rise to hadrosaurs that had thousands of highly specialized teeth for grinding vegetation. Hadrosaurs were incredibly successful and spread out across Laurasia, dispersing across oceans to South America and Africa toward the end of the Cretaceous.

Both marginocephalian groups—the pachycephalosaurs and ceratopsians—diversified throughout the Cretaceous. Pachycephalosaurs developed elaborate ornamented domes and spread throughout Asia and North America. Ceratopsians remained small until the Late Cretaceous, when they increased in size, exploded in diversity, and formed vast herds that roamed across North America. Some of the big Late Cretaceous ceratopsians, such as *Torosaurus*, had the largest skulls of any land animal. Ceratopsians also developed a complex battery of teeth, but they employed a slicing method of chewing. Two groups of ceratopsians evolved: the ornately frilled centrosaurines, and the long-horned chasmosaurines. Neither of these groups would ever reach Asia, but the reason for this remains unclear.

Group: ANKYLOSAURIA	Subgroup: Ankylosauridae	Time: 68–66 mya

Ankylosaurus

AN-KIE-LOH-SAW-RUS

Ankylosaurus ("fused lizard") has aptly been described as a living tank. Its stocky body, neck, and head were protected by thick bands of armor plating. The skin was thick and leathery and was studded with hundreds of oval bony plates and rows of spikes. A pair of long spikes stuck out from the back of the head, and the cheekbones were drawn out into another pair of spikes on the face. The tail was armed with a bony club, which could be swung with great force. The legs were strong, although short, and the body was wide and squat. The face was also broad, with a blunt snout that ended in a toothless beak.

DESCRIBED BY Brown 1908
HABITAT Woodland

bony plates

horny beak

front legs shorter than hind legs

Length: 25–35 ft (7.5–10.5 m)	Weight: 4⅜–6⅞ tons (4.5–7 metric tons)	Diet: Plants

Group: THYREOPHORA	Subgroup: Ankylosauria	Time: 105–99 mya

Kunbarrasaurus

KOON-BAR-AH-SAW-RUS

This small, heavily built, and thickly armored ankylosaur is named for the Mayi (language of the Wunumara indigenous people of Queensland, Australia) word for "shield." It had rows of small, bony plates running down its back and triangular spikes over the hips. There were also large, bony plates over the neck and shoulders. The head was box-shaped, with a very narrow snout ending in a horny beak. Four small horns jutted out from the back of the face.

DESCRIBED BY Leahey et al. 2015
HABITAT Shrubby and wooded plains

short neck

short, sturdy legs

wide feet

Length: 9¾ ft (3 m)	Weight: Not calculated	Diet: Low-lying vegetation

large, bony tail club

terminal plate

end of tail held out stiffly

lateral plate

feet with five short toes

nostril

head spike

bony tendons to support end of tail

unprotected underbelly

teeth   **Fossil skull**

Fossil tail club

Group: ANKYLOSAURIA	Subgroup: Ankylosauridae	Time: 144–112 mya

Gastonia

GAS-TONE-EE-A

curved dorsal spines

Gastonia (named after paleontologist and castmaker Robert Gaston) had a mixture of ankylosaur and nodosaur features. This herbivore's defensive armor was impressive: there were four horns on the head and bony rings covering the neck; rows of spikes covered the back and the flanks; and fused, bony armored plates protected the hips. The tail, which could lash from side to side, had rows of triangular blades along each side. Running down both sides of the spine, long spikes curved up and outward, forming a formidable defensive shield against attack by predators.

horny beak

DESCRIBED BY Kirkland 1998
HABITAT Woodland

Length: 16 ft (5 m)	Weight: ~1 ton (1 metric ton)	Diet: Plants

Group: ANKYLOSAURIA	Subgroup: Ankylosauridae	Time: 77–76 mya

Euoplocephalus

YOU-OH-PLO-SEF-AH-LUSS

skull highest in front of eyes

bony spikes and studs along back

large nasal cavity

Fossil skull

Built like a military tank, the back of *Euoplocephalus* ("well-armored head") was embedded with bands of armor and bony studs. Fused plates covered the neck and triangular horns protected the shoulders, base of the tail, and face. A large ball of fused bone at the end of the tail acted as a club that could be swung at attacking predators.

DESCRIBED BY Lambe 1910
HABITAT Woodland

secondary bony eyelids protected eyes

short, stumpy limbs

Length: 20 ft (6 m)	Weight: ~2¼ tons (2 metric tons)	Diet: Plants

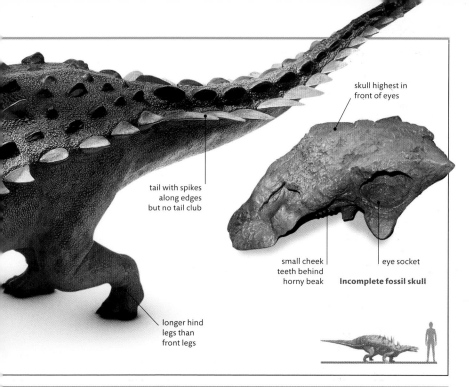

skull highest in front of eyes

tail with spikes along edges but no tail club

small cheek teeth behind horny beak

eye socket

Incomplete fossil skull

longer hind legs than front legs

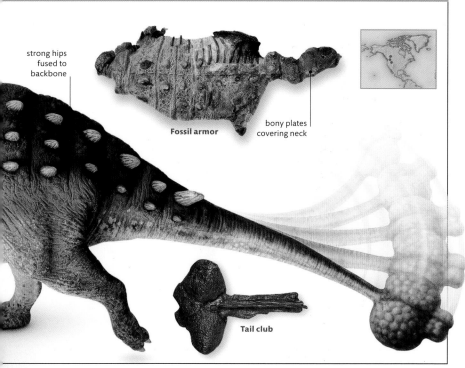

strong hips fused to backbone

Fossil armor

bony plates covering neck

Tail club

Group: ANKYLOSAURIA	Subgroup: Nodosauridae	Time: 73–71 mya

Edmontonia

ED-MON-TONE-EE-AH

This ankylosaur (whose name means "from Edmonton") had a bulky body; four short, thick legs; wide feet; and a short neck. The back and tail were covered with rows of bony plates (scutes) and spikes. The shoulders of this dinosaur were particularly well-armored with long spikes and large scutes. Fossil scutes that have been found are not symmetrical, meaning that they would not have projected straight out from the hide, but at an angle. *Edmontonia*'s skull was long and flat, with large nasal cavities and weak jaws. The front of the snout was formed into a horny, toothless beak, with small, weak cheek teeth inside the mouth. Some paleontologists have suggested that *Edmontonia* is more likely to have used its shoulder spikes for defense or sexual display than for combat.

DESCRIBED BY Sternberg 1928
HABITAT Woodland

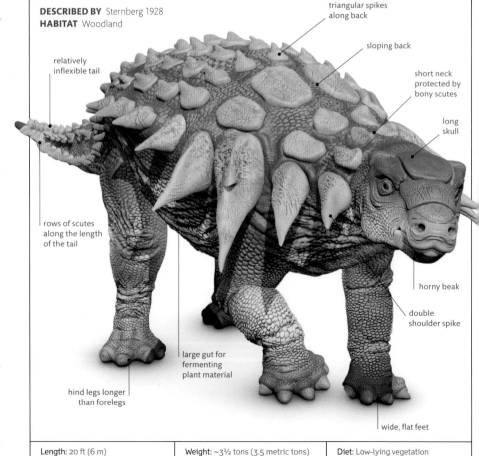

triangular spikes along back

sloping back

short neck protected by bony scutes

long skull

relatively inflexible tail

rows of scutes along the length of the tail

horny beak

double shoulder spike

large gut for fermenting plant material

hind legs longer than forelegs

wide, flat feet

Length: 20 ft (6 m)	Weight: ~3½ tons (3.5 metric tons)	Diet: Low-lying vegetation

Group: MARGINOCEPHALIA	Subgroup: Pachycephalosauria	Time: 77–76 mya

Stegoceras

STEG-OH-SER-AS

A fast runner, *Stegoceras* (meaning "roof horn") had a body designed to withstand vigorous head-butting activity. When charging, its head was lowered at right angles, balanced by its neck, body, and tail held in a straight line. The skullcap was thickened into a dome of solid bone, and the grain of bone was angled to the surface, enabling it to withstand impact more effectively. Two types of skull have been found—some with low, flat domes and others with tall, rounded ones. These variations probably reflect differences between juveniles and adults. *Stegoceras* had small, serrated teeth that were ideal for shredding plant material.

DESCRIBED BY Lambe 1902
HABITAT Upland forests

ridge of bone over eye and around back of head

skullcap thickened into dome of bone

Fossil skull

slightly curved, serrated teeth

domed skull

neck designed to be held horizontally when charging

expanded chamber at base of tail had unknown function

bony frill extended from back of skull

long, slim arms

three long, forward-facing, clawed toes

Length: 6½ ft (2 m)	Weight: ~120 lb (54 kg)	Diet: Leaves, fruit

| Group: MARGINOCEPHALIA | Subgroup: Pachycephalosauria | Time: 70–66 mya |

Pachycephalosaurus

PACK-EE-SEF-AL-OH-SAW-RUS

It is easy to see why *Pachycephalosaurus* ("thick-headed lizard") was so named. The top of the dinosaur's skull was thickened into a dome of solid bone 10 in (25 cm) thick. It is thought that *Pachycephalosaurus* used its head as a battering ram for defense or in territorial fighting. It had a beak, and clusters of bony knobs surrounded the snout. Further groups of round knobs encircled the back of the head. Its relatively slim leg and foot bones indicate that this dinosaur may have been able to run more quickly than its heavy build might suggest. *Pachycephalosaurus* is the largest member of the Pachycephalosauridae family of dinosaurs discovered so far and was the last to exist before the extinction of the dinosaurs at the end of the Cretaceous Period.

DESCRIBED BY Brown and Schlaikjer 1943
HABITAT Forests

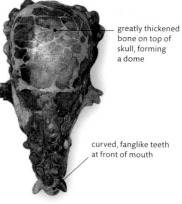

greatly thickened bone on top of skull, forming a dome

curved, fanglike teeth at front of mouth

Skull

straight tail stiffened by ligaments

bony protuberances around back of head

small, horny bumps covering the nose

five-fingered hands

long, slim legs

long claws

three-toed feet

| Length: 16 ft (5 m) | Weight: ~2¼ tons (2 metric tons) | Diet: Leaves, fruit, possibly small animals |

Group: MARGINOCEPHALIA	Subgroup: Ceratopsia	Time: 126–101 mya

Psittacosaurus

SIT-A-KOH-SAW-RUS

Its characteristic square skull and curved beak were the features that led to this dinosaur being given its name, which means "parrot lizard." Its cheekbones formed a pair of horns, believed to have been used for fighting or sexual display. Its hind legs were long and thin, suggesting that it was a fast bipedal runner. The long toes with blunt claws were possibly used for digging. Its long tail was stiffened by bony tendons along its length.

DESCRIBED BY Osborn 1923
HABITAT Desert and shrubland

teeth behind toothless beak

horn

Fossil skull

tail to maintain balance

four clawed toes on hind feet

Length: 6¼ ft (2 m)	Weight: ~175 lb (80 kg)	Diet: Plants

Group: MARGINOCEPHALIA	Subgroup: Ceratopsia	Time: 83–76 mya

Protoceratops

PRO-TOE-SER-A-TOPS

Protoceratops ("before the horned faces") is very well-known from the many specimens discovered. It had a broad neck frill at the back of its skull. There was a small nasal horn between the eyes and numerous teeth in the upper jaw, similar to other ceratopsians. *Protoceratops* had slender legs and was unlikely to have been a fast runner.

head frill, which grew with age

hump in tail for display or for fat storage

Adult skull

DESCRIBED BY Granger and Gregory 1923
HABITAT Shrubland and desert

slender legs

Length: 6 ft (1.8 m)	Weight: ~400 lb (180 kg)	Diet: Plants

| Group: CERATOPSIA | Subgroup: Centrosaurinae | Time: 77–76 mya |

Centrosaurus

SEN-TROH-SAW-RUS

The most distinctive feature of *Centrosaurus* ("pointed lizard") was the long horn on the snout. There were also two small brow horns and a neck frill standing up behind the head. This neck frill had a wavy edge and spines. *Centrosaurus* had a massive body, a short tail, and sturdy legs. Many *Centrosaurus* and *Styracosaurus* have been found together in a single bone bed, having died during a drought around a watering hole.

DESCRIBED BY Lambe 1904
HABITAT Woodland

wavy edge

brow horn for display and defense

skin-covered holes to reduce weight of neck frill

saw-edged teeth

horny beak

| Length: 20 ft (6 m) | Weight: ~3 tons (3 tonnes) | Diet: Low-lying plants |

| Group: CERATOPSIA | Subgroup: Centrosaurinae | Time: 77–76 mya |

Styracosaurus

STY-RAK-OH-SAW-RUS

One of the most spectacular of the horned lizards, *Styracosaurus* ("spiked lizard") had six long spikes on the back edge of its neck frill and smaller spikes around them. There was a large horn on the snout that pointed upward and forward. Its snout was very deep and its nostrils seem to have been unusually large, although the reason for this is unknown. All four feet had five fingers or toes with clawlike hooves. Its teeth grew continuously to replace worn ones and had a shearing action for slicing through tough plant material.

DESCRIBED BY Lambe 1913
HABITAT Open woodland

holes in neck frill to reduce weight

defensive spikes

Fossil skull

defensive horn on snout

| Length: 17 ft (5.2 m) | Weight: ~2¾ tons (2.8 metric tons) | Diet: Ferns and cycads |

Group: CERATOPSIA	Subgroup: Chasmosaurinae	Time: 77–76 mya

Chasmosaurus

KAZ-MOH-SAW-RUS

Chasmosaurus ("opening lizard") was a typical frilled, horned dinosaur. It had a large body with four stocky legs. Its most distinctive feature—its enormous neck frill—was likely to have been brightly colored in life for sexual display. The frill was so long that it reached over the shoulders. Its bony structure was lightened by two large holes that were covered with skin. Triangular, bony protrusions ran along the edge of the frill. *Chasmosaurus* had a small nose horn and two blunt brow horns that were of different lengths in different species or sexes. There was also a parrotlike beak at the front of the snout. The skin was covered in knoblike bumps with five or six sides.

DESCRIBED BY Lambe 1914
HABITAT Woodland

bony protrusions along frill edge

large nasal cavity

Front view of skull

hips firmly attached by eight sacral vertebrae

neck frill held upright, possibly to scare predators

short tail

blunt hooves

five short toes on all four feet

horny, parrotlike beak

Length: 16 ft (5 m)	Weight: ~2½ tons (2.5 metric tons)	Diet: Cycads, palms, other plants

Group: CERATOPSIA	Subgroup: Chasmosaurinae	Time: 68–66 mya

Triceratops

TRY-SER-A-TOPS

Probably the best-known of the horned dinosaurs, *Triceratops* (meaning three-horned face") lived throughout the lands that now form North America at the end of the Cretaceous Period. The nose horn was short and thick, and the two long brow horns, each over 3¼ ft (1 m) long, curved forward and slightly outward over the snout. There were pointed studs set around the edge of the neck frill for further protection and ornamentation. Many of the fossil skulls found have evidence of scarring. This suggests that *Triceratops* may have fought in territorial or mating battles by locking horns with rivals.

DESCRIBED BY Marsh 1889
HABITAT Woodland

TRICERATOPS SKULL

The solid structure of *Triceratops*'s skull has meant that it survived fossilization better than most other dinosaur skulls. More than 50 *Triceratops* skulls have been found to date.

horny beak at front of snout

solid neck frill

Length: 30 ft (9 m)	Weight: ~4⅜–9⅞ tons (4.5–10 metric tons)	Diet: Plants

strong pelvic structure

short nose horn

head joined to neck by ball and socket joint

Reconstruction of skeleton

bony studs around margin of frill

heavy frill of solid bone

brow horns much longer than nose horn

Group: CERATOPSIA	Subgroup: Chasmosaurinae	Time: 75–73 mya

Pentaceratops

PEN-TAH-SER-A-TOPS

Pentaceratops ("five-horn face") was so named because, in addition to the usual straight horn on the snout and two curved brow horns, its cheeks had spikelike protrusions. *Pentaceratops's* most unusual feature is the size of its head—a skull reconstructed in 1998 was over 7.6 ft (2.3 m) long. Its neck frill was also enormous and edged with triangular, bony projections. The body was stockily built, with a short, pointed tail; a wide body; and hooflike claws.

Skull fragment

DESCRIBED BY Osborn 1923
HABITAT Wooded plains

scalloped edges on neck frill

large neck frill, possibly elaborately colored for sexual display

heavily built body with thick hide

curved brow horns longer in males

straight nose horn

cheek horn

short legs

curved beak made of horn

hooflike claws

Length: 16–26 ft (5–8 m)	Weight: ~2½–9 tons (2.5–8 metric tons)	Diet: Plants

Group: ORNITHISCHIA	Subgroup: Ornithopoda	Time: 132–129 mya

Hypsilophodon

HIP-SILL-OH-FO-DON

This primitive ornithischian, whose name means "*Hypsilophus* tooth," is generally believed to have been a fully terrestrial dinosaur that was capable of running at high speeds. It walked on its hind legs; its short thigh bones and long shins meant that it was capable of taking long strides. The tail, stiffened by a network of bony ligaments, helped balance the animal as it ran. Its small head had a horny beak and large eyes. The jaws held 28 or 30 cheek teeth that were self-sharpening, and the mouth had cheek pouches. Groups of fossils found together in bone beds suggest that this was a herding dinosaur.

DESCRIBED BY Huxley 1869
HABITAT Forests

possibly two rows of bony plates down back

slightly built skeleton

five-fingered hands

four-toed feet, one with claw

small beak

short, relatively weak forelimbs

slim tail held out straight behind body

Length: 6½ ft (2 m)	Weight: ~150 lb (68 kg)	Diet: Plants

Group: ORNITHOPODA	Subgroup: Iguanodontia	Time: 132–129 mya

Iguanodon

IG-WAH-NOH-DON

Iguanodon ("iguana tooth") was thought to have been capable of bipedal walking, but recent analysis suggests that it was strictly quadrupedal. Its hind legs were thick and columnlike, while the front legs were considerably shorter and thinner. The middle three fingers on each hand were joined together by a pad of skin and the fifth finger could curl to grasp food. The thumb was armed with a long spike. *Iguanodon* could chew food; it had a hinged upper jaw that allowed the teeth in the upper jaw to grind over those in the lower jaw.

DESCRIBED BY Mantell 1825
HABITAT Woodland

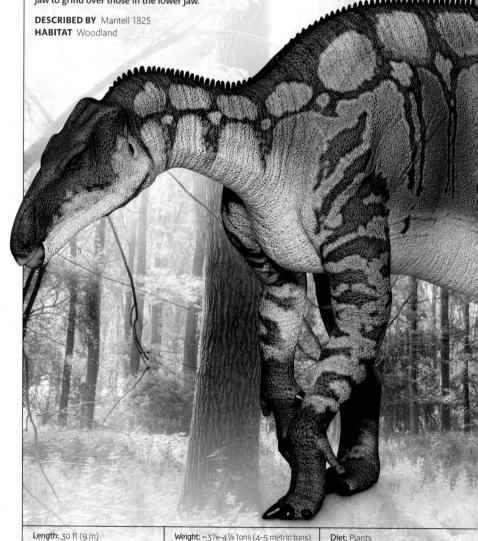

Length: 30 ft (9 m)	Weight: ~3⅞–4⅞ tons (4–5 metric tons)	Diet: Plants

batteries of grinding
cheek teeth

horny beak
at front
of jaw

Fossil skull

body held
horizontally and
balanced at hips

6-in (15-cm)
long thumb spike

Fossil thumb spike

deep tail held stiffly
out for balance

Group: ORNITHOPODA	Subgroup: Iguanodontia	Time: 129–125 mya

Ouranosaurus

OO-RAH-NOH-SAW-RUS

The most remarkable feature of *Ouranosaurus*, whose name means "brave lizard," was the row of spines growing out from the spinal and caudal vertebrae. They ran from the shoulders to halfway along the tail. Some paleontologists think they supported a sail that was most likely used for sexual display. *Ouranosaurus* had a pair of bony bumps between the eyes and a horny beak.

DESCRIBED BY Taquet 1972
HABITAT Tropical plains and forest

pair of bony bumps formed head crest

horny beak

thumb spike

Length: 23 ft (7 m)	Weight: ~4 tons (4 tonnes)	Diet: Leaves, fruit, seeds

Group: HADROSAURIDAE	Subgroup: Saurolophinae	Time: 83–70 mya

Maiasaura

MAY-A-SAW-RA

This dinosaur's name means "good mother lizard." It was so named because remains were found close to fossilized nests scooped out of mud. The nests were each about 6½ ft (2 m) across and contained eggs arranged in circular layers. Remains of juvenile dinosaurs at various stages of development showed that the parents brought food to their young at the nest site for a considerable time. It appears that *Maiasaura* nested each year in large herds. It had numerous cheek teeth adapted to grinding tough plant material.

DESCRIBED BY Horner and Makela 1979
HABITAT Coastal plains

stiff, narrow tail

long hind legs

Skeleton of juvenile

Length: 30 ft (9 m)	Weight: ~4⅞ tons (5 metric tons)	Diet: Leaves

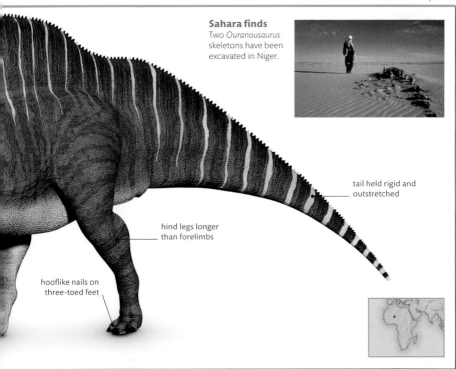

Sahara finds
Two *Ouranosaurus* skeletons have been excavated in Niger.

tail held rigid and outstretched

hind legs longer than forelimbs

hooflike nails on three-toed feet

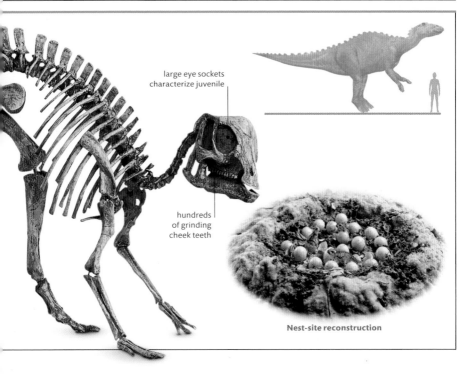

large eye sockets characterize juvenile

hundreds of grinding cheek teeth

Nest-site reconstruction

Group: HADROSAURIDAE	Subgroup: Lambeosaurinae	Time: 77–76 mya

Corythosaurus

KOH-RITH-OH-SAW-RUS

Corythosaurus ("Corinthian helmet lizard") was named for the distinctive hollow crest on top of its head. The crest was made up of greatly altered nasal bones, and the hollows were expanded nasal passages. Models of the crest have been made, which produce a booming foghornlike sound when blown through, adding to the current theory that the crest served as a resonating device for signaling among herds. *Corythosaurus* was a low browser that spent most of its time on all fours. It had a broad, toothless beak.

vertebral spines possibly supported narrow skin frill

spectacular head crest

sigmoid neck held head close to ground

DESCRIBED BY
Brown 1914
HABITAT Forests

Length: 33 ft (10 m)	Weight: ~5 tons (4.5 metric tons)	Diet: Leaves, seeds, pine needles

Group: HADROSAURIDAE	Subgroup: Lambeosaurinae	Time: 77–73 mya

Parasaurolophus

PA-RA-SAW-ROL-OFF-US

This dinosaur, whose name means "near *Saurolophus*," is instantly recognizable from its trombonelike head crest. This was up to 6 ft (1.8 m) long and was probably used for display and as a resonating device for sound signaling. It was thought that a frill of skin connected the crest to the neck, but this is now considered unlikely.

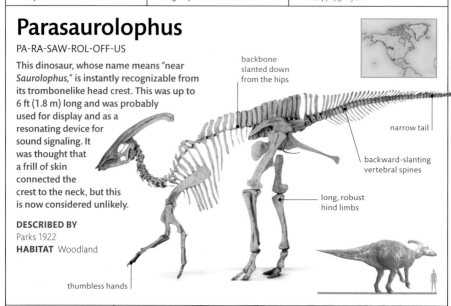

backbone slanted down from the hips

narrow tail

backward-slanting vertebral spines

long, robust hind limbs

thumbless hands

DESCRIBED BY
Parks 1922
HABITAT Woodland

Length: 33 ft (10 m)	Weight: ~4½ tons (4 metric tons)	Diet: Leaves, seeds, pine needles

tall vertebral spines and chevrons in tail area

top vertebral spines slanted backward

tail stiffened by network of bony ligaments

relatively short toes

Detail of hip region
The network of bony rods on *Corythosaurus*'s tail kept the backbone immobile.

Group: HADROSAURIDAE	Subgroup: Lambeosaurinae	Time: 77–76 mya

Lambeosaurus

LAM-BEE-OH-SAW-RUS

hollow crest for signaling

Fossil skull

Lambeosaurus, named after paleontologist Lawrence Lambe, was closely related to *Corythosaurus*. It was unusual in having two distinctive head structures: a tall, hollow crest leaning over the snout and a solid, backward-pointing spike of bone behind it. These were probably used for social recognition and signaling. Like other members of this family, it had a deep, narrow tail, held stiff and immobile. The animal moved around in large herds, browsing on low-growing vegetation on all fours.

DESCRIBED BY
Parker 1923
HABITAT Woodland

bony spike

spine slanted downward from the hip

tall vertebral spines and chevrons forming long, deep tail

Length: 30 ft (9 m)	Weight: ~4½ tons (4 metric tons)	Diet: Low-growing leaves, fruit, seeds

OTHER DIAPSIDS

AS FOR MOST OTHER groups of animals, the Cretaceous was a peak in diversity for many of the diapsids.

Turtles returned to the sea, and some, such as *Archelon*, reached gigantic sizes. Lepidosaurs diversified, and in the Late Cretaceous the first snakes appeared. At around the same time, a close relative of snakes returned to the water and gave rise to the mosasaurs, which would become the top predators in the seas. They were able to do so partly because ichthyosaurs had declined in number, eventually going extinct prior to the Cretaceous-Paleogene extinction.

Pliosaurs and plesiosaurs remained top aquatic predators throughout the Early Cretaceous, and continued to specialize. While the pliosaurs remained short-necked and developed enormous skulls to take down large prey, the plesiosaurs elongated their necks, culminating in the elasmosaurids, some with more than 70 vertebrae in the neck.

Throughout the Early Cretaceous, pterodactyloid pterosaurs radiated into a wide array of highly specialized forms. Some, such as *Quetzalcoatlus* (see p.154), reached incredible sizes unparalleled by any other flying animals. It was believed that pterosaurs declined in diversity in the Late Cretaceous, with only large-bodied lineages surviving, possibly as a result of competition with birds. However, numerous new studies show that small pterosaurs survived, only going extinct with the dinosaurs at the end of the Cretaceous.

Group: PLESIOSAURIA	Subgroup: Pliosauroidea	Time: 125–100 mya

Kronosaurus
CRO-NO-SAW-RUS

Kronosaurus ("Kronos lizard") was a giant marine reptile, classed as a pliosaur because of its enormous head, compact body, and short neck and tail. Fossilized stomach contents show that *Kronosaurus* lived similar to a modern shark, devouring anything that came its way. Its head alone was 9¾ ft (3 m) long, and its sharp, pointed teeth were about 10 in (25 cm) long. Its snout was long and triangular. It had two pairs of flippers, the rear ones being longer than the front pair. There may have been a fin at the top of the tail to help steer the animal. The body of *Kronosaurus* was kept stiff as it swam by tightly linked belly ribs (gastralia).

short tail

large rear flippers

DESCRIBED BY Longman 1924
HABITAT Deep oceans

Length: 33 ft (10 m)	Weight: ~7 tons (7 metric tons)	Diet: Marine reptiles, fish, mollusks

Group: DIAPSIDA	Subgroup: Testudines	Time: 80–74 mya

Archelon

AR-KAY-LON

This marine animal, whose name means "ruling turtle," was twice the length of modern species. It had a wide, flattened shell. This was formed from belly ribs (gastralia) that grew out from the body wall. The shell was composed of a leathery covering or horny plates over a framework of bony struts that may have been visible underneath.

DESCRIBED BY Wieland 1896
HABITAT Oceans

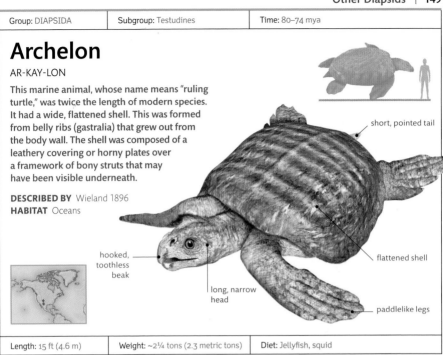

short, pointed tail

flattened shell

hooked, toothless beak

long, narrow head

paddlelike legs

Length: 15 ft (4.6 m)	Weight: ~2¼ tons (2.3 metric tons)	Diet: Jellyfish, squid

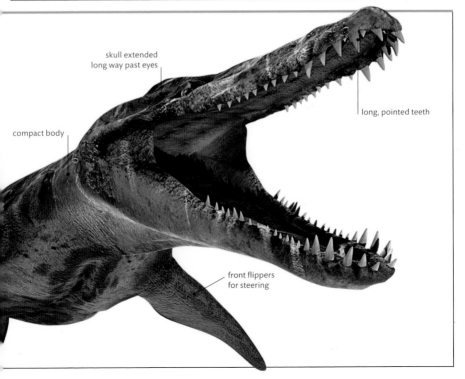

skull extended long way past eyes

long, pointed teeth

compact body

front flippers for steering

Group: PLESIOSAURIA	Subgroup: Plesiosauroidea	Time: 84–72 mya

Elasmosaurus

EH-LAZ-MOH-SAW-RUS

Elasmosaurus ("ribbon lizard") was the longest known plesiosaur. More than half of its body length consisted of the greatly elongated neck. This had 72 vertebrae, whereas earlier plesiosaurs had only 28. The length and structure of its neck meant that *Elasmosaurus* would have been able to snatch prey from a wide area around its head. It was earlier also thought to have held its neck high above water to spot prey. However, the idea is no longer supported, as *Elasmosaurus*'s center of gravity would have limited its ability to raise its head too far out the water except when its body was in contact with the seabed. *Elasmosaurus*'s body was similar to that of other plesiosaurs: it had four long, paddlelike flippers; a tiny head; sharp teeth in strong jaws; and a short, pointed tail.

DESCRIBED BY Cope 1868
HABITAT Oceans

greatly elongated neck

tiny head and mouth with small, sharp teeth

Length: 46 ft (14 m)	Weight: ~3¼ tons (3 metric tons)	Diet: Fish, squid, shellfish

front flippers
slightly longer
than hind ones

short, stiff body

short, pointed tail

Lepidotes

Elasmosaurus feasted on large fish such as *Lepidotes* (right) and many other forms of marine life that abounded in the Cretaceous oceans. *Lepidotes* was almost the length of a human and was itself a voracious predator of smaller marine creatures, such as shellfish, which it crushed with its strong teeth.

bony rays
supported
each fin

rigid
overlapping
scales

Group: SQUAMATA	Subgroup: Mosasauridae	Time: 93–66 mya

Tylosaurus

TIE-LOW-SAW-RUS

This large sea lizard was one of the later members of the mosasaur family and a fearsome predator. It had teeth on its palate bones, as well as those in its long jaws. Its skull bones could move quite freely at the joints, allowing it to expand its jaws to swallow large prey. The snout was hard and bony at the tip (its name means "knob lizard"), leading some paleontologists to surmise that it may have rammed its prey. *Tylosaurus* probably swam by moving its deep, narrow tail in a side-to-side motion and steering with its large, wing-shaped flippers.

DESCRIBED BY Marsh 1872
HABITAT Shallow seas

long, slim snout

powerful jaws capable of smashing turtle shells and bones

Length: 46 ft (14 m)	Weight: ~6⅞ tons (7 tonnes)	Diet: Turtles, fish, other mosasaurs

Group: SQUAMATA	Subgroup: Mosasauridae	Time: 83–66 mya

Mosasaurus

MOH-SAH-SAW-RUS

This marine lizard, named for the Meuse River, was the first giant reptile ever to be named. It was one of the largest mosasaurs, with a slender, cylindrical barrel-like body; a long, powerful tail; and four long, paddlelike limbs. Its skull was strong, and the jaws contained many backward-curving teeth capable of crushing and cutting. Healed injuries on fossil remains indicate that *Mosasaurus* lived a violent lifestyle. It is likely to have been a surface-swimming animal.

DESCRIBED BY
Conybeare 1822
HABITAT Oceans

long, flattened tail moved from side to side

streamlined body

paddlelike limbs

rosette of teeth

Length: 40–59 ft (12.5–18 m)	Weight: ~40 tons (40 metric tons)	Diet: Squid, fish, shellfish

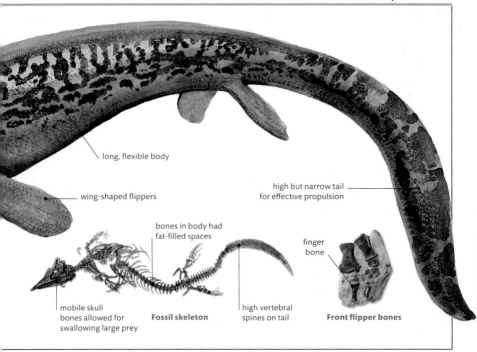

long, flexible body

wing-shaped flippers

high but narrow tail
for effective propulsion

bones in body had
fat-filled spaces

finger
bone

mobile skull
bones allowed for
swallowing large prey

Fossil skeleton

high vertebral
spines on tail

Front flipper bones

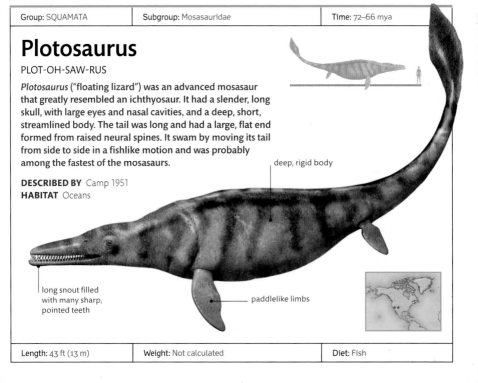

Group: SQUAMATA	Subgroup: Mosasauridae	Time: 72–66 mya

Plotosaurus

PLOT-OH-SAW-RUS

Plotosaurus ("floating lizard") was an advanced mosasaur
that greatly resembled an ichthyosaur. It had a slender, long
skull, with large eyes and nasal cavities, and a deep, short,
streamlined body. The tail was long and had a large, flat end
formed from raised neural spines. It swam by moving its tail
from side to side in a fishlike motion and was probably
among the fastest of the mosasaurs.

DESCRIBED BY Camp 1951
HABITAT Oceans

deep, rigid body

long snout filled
with many sharp,
pointed teeth

paddlelike limbs

Length: 43 ft (13 m)	Weight: Not calculated	Diet: Fish

Group: PTEROSAURIA	Subgroup: Pterodactyloidea	Time: 125–100 mya

Pterodaustro

TER-OH-DAS-TROH

The most remarkable feature of this large pterodactyl was its long, curved jaws. The lower jaw contained thousands of very thin teeth, which were probably used to sieve plankton. The upper teeth were used to comb out the lower teeth.

DESCRIBED BY
Bonaparte 1970
HABITAT
Seashores, lakes

large feet for
a pterosaur

large wingspan
of 4 ft (1.2 m)

elongated
fourth finger
supported wing

bristlelike
lower teeth

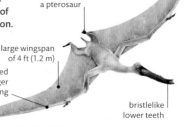

Length: 4 ft (1.3 m)	Weight: Not calculated	Diet: Plankton

Group: PTERODACTYLOIDEA	Subgroup: Pteranodontia	Time: 86–84 mya

Pteranodon

TER-AN-OH-DON

Pteranodon was one of the largest pterodactyls. It probably flapped its wings to get off the ground and spent a lot of time soaring, actively flapping when necessary. The long crest on its head was probably used for sexual display.

DESCRIBED BY
Marsh 1876
HABITAT
Oceans, shores

wingspan
of 23 ft (7 m)

long, toothless
jaws possibly used
to scoop up fish

feet likely to
have been
webbed

Length: 6 ft (1.8 m)	Weight: ~35 lb (16 kg)	Diet: Fish

Group: PTERODACTYLOIDEA	Subgroup: Azhdarchoidea	Time: 68–66 mya

Quetzalcoatlus

KWET-ZAL-KOH-AT-LUS

Remains of *Quetzalcoatlus*, indicating a wingspan of 36 ft (11 m), show it to have been the largest flying vertebrate known to date. Its wings were narrow and relatively inflexible. There was a small, bony crest on the head.

DESCRIBED BY
Lawson 1975
HABITAT All

long,
inflexible
neck

toothless
jaws

long,
narrow
wings

vestigial
tail

Length: 25 ft (7.5 m)	Weight: ~190 lb (86 kg)	Diet: Freshwater arthropods, carrion

| Group: PTERODACTYLOIDEA | Subgroup: Pteranodontia | Time: 119–100 mya |

Tropeognathus

TROH-PEE-OH-NAY-THUS

Tropeognathus's most striking feature was the distinctive bulbous bony keel at the end of its long snout, which led to its name ("keel jaw"). This was probably patterned and was used for signaling purposes or sexual display. This fish-eating pterosaur had a short tail and neck–typical features of its group. As in other pterosaurs, the wings were formed from thin membranous skin stretched between the elongated fourth fingers and the ankles. The body may have been covered in dense hair.

DESCRIBED BY Wellnhofer 1987
HABITAT Oceans, shores

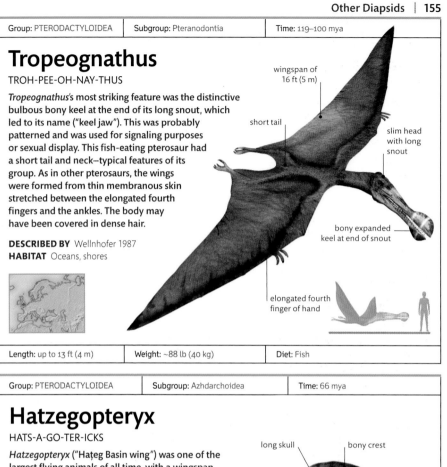

wingspan of 16 ft (5 m)

short tail

slim head with long snout

bony expanded keel at end of snout

elongated fourth finger of hand

| Length: up to 13 ft (4 m) | Weight: ~88 lb (40 kg) | Diet: Fish |

| Group: PTERODACTYLOIDEA | Subgroup: Azhdarchoidea | Time: 66 mya |

Hatzegopteryx

HATS-A-GO-TER-ICKS

Hatzegopteryx ("Hațeg Basin wing") was one of the largest flying animals of all time, with a wingspan of nearly 39 ft (12 m). Unlike other pterosaurs, which were lightly built, *Hatzegopteryx* had bulky bones and a short neck, suggesting that it would have been a fearsome, powerful predator. It was probably the apex predator of the Hațeg Basin, which at the time was an isolated island with no large land predators.

DESCRIBED BY
Buffetaut et al. 2002
HABITAT Offshore islands

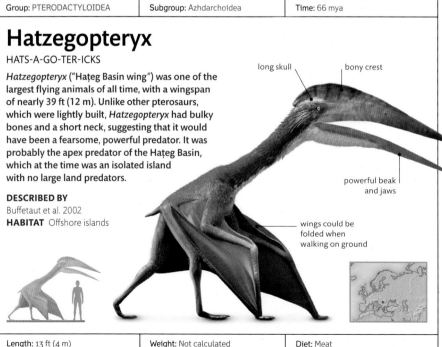

long skull

bony crest

powerful beak and jaws

wings could be folded when walking on ground

| Length: 13 ft (4 m) | Weight: Not calculated | Diet: Meat |

MAMMALS

AS IN THE JURASSIC, the mammals of the Cretaceous were relatively small but ecologically diverse. The multituberculates, which had evolved in the Jurassic, became globally widespread and abundant. This was enabled by their peculiar, efficient chewing apparatus—rodentlike incisors, and a large, bladelike premolar, with several rectangular molars designed for grinding. Triconodontids, another early-branching mammal group, were also successful, and some, such as the badger-sized *Repenomamus*, even preyed on small dinosaurs.

The only mammals that survive today, however, are from lineages that converged independently upon a key adaptation—complex molars that could both crush and shear in the same bite. One of these groups, from the southern hemisphere, gave rise to the monotremes, represented today by the platypus and the echidnas. The other group, from the northern hemisphere, split into the eutherians (ancestors of the placentals, including humans) and metatherians (ancestors of marsupials).

In the mid-Cretaceous, eutherians and metatherians diversified together with the rise of angiosperms and their pollinators. Eutherians were relatively small, specialized components of ecosystems, contrasting their ubiquity today. Instead, metatherians such as *Didelphodon* were far more widespread in the Cretaceous than they are today, and were the dominant mammals, alongside multituberculates, in Late Cretaceous ecosystems of Laurasia.

Group: MAMMALIA	Subgroup: Eutheria	Time: 83–76 mya

Zalambdalestes

ZAH-LAMB-DAL-ES-TEES

Zalambdalestes was a shrewlike mammal, with a long tail and powerful hind legs that were longer than the front ones. The legs had elongated foot bones and the hands were small, with nonopposable fingers. This suggests that *Zalambdalestes* was probably not a tree dweller. The eyes were very large and the snout turned up sharply at the end. The incisors were long and sharp. The recent discovery of an epipubic bone (present only in nonplacental mammals) in a skeleton of *Zalambdalestes* means it is considered a transitional form of mammal.

sensitive, long, upturned snout

DESCRIBED BY
Gregory and Simpson 1926
HABITAT Prairie

Length: 8 in (20 cm)	Weight: ~1 oz (25 g)	Diet: Insects

Group: MAMMALIA	Subgroup: Metatheria	Time: 72–66 mya

Didelphodon

DIE-DEL-FOE-DON

Didelphodon was one of the largest Mesozoic mammals. A heavily built lower jaw and powerful teeth suggest that it had an incredibly strong bite for its size. *Didelphodon* could likely crush bones or shells with its bite, so it may have been both a predator and a scavenger, feeding on small prey, carrion, and molluscs. However, wear patterns on its teeth suggest that it supplemented its diet with insects and plants.

Elongated, otterlike body, possibly semi-aquatic

DESCRIBED BY
Marsh 1889
HABITAT Swamps, floodplains, and riverbanks

small braincase

heavily built jaw for a crushing bite

Length: 3 ft (1 m)	Weight: ~11 lb (5 kg)	Diet: Small prey, carrion, and molluscs

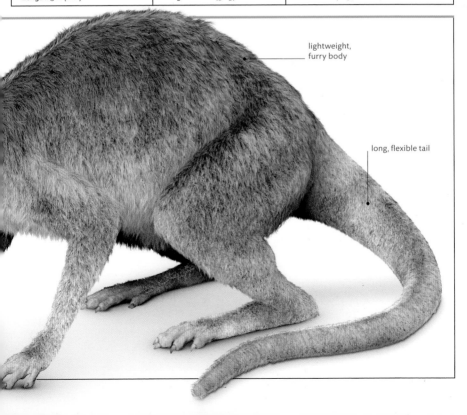

lightweight, furry body

long, flexible tail

CENOZOIC ERA
AGE OF MAMMALS

The Cenozoic Era (comprising the Paleogene, Neogene, and Quaternary Periods) followed the end-Cretaceous mass extinction event, which marked the disappearance of the dinosaurs, pterosaurs, some birds and mammals, and many marine species.

During the Paleogene (Paleocene, Eocene, and Oligocene Epochs), the surviving mammals and birds diversified rapidly to take over the ecological niches left vacant by the dinosaurs. During the Neogene (Miocene and Pliocene Epochs), the spread of grasslands led to the evolution of modern forms of grazing mammals.

By the Quaternary Period (Pleistocene and Holocene Epochs), animal and plant life generally resembled modern forms, although some species that were adapted to recurring ice ages did not survive into modern times.

PALEOGENE PERIOD

66–23 MILLION YEARS AGO

THE PALEOGENE, including the Paleocene, Eocene, and Oligocene Epochs, was the beginning of the "Age of Mammals." Many ecological niches had been left vacant by the end-Cretaceous mass extinction of dinosaurs, and mammal and bird populations evolved and expanded rapidly to fill the gaps. Climates worldwide were warm or hot, with high rainfall. Vast areas of swampy forest and tropical rainforest developed. Toward the end of the Eocene, a large ice cap formed over the South Pole. This resulted in a fall in sea levels, and the climate became much cooler. Tropical forests disappeared in temperate regions and were replaced by woodlands dominated by deciduous and coniferous trees.

PALEOGENE LIFE

Despite the rapid evolution of mammals into many ecological niches, large herbivores only appeared at the end of the Paleocene (about 53 mya). There were some large mammalian carnivores, notably the mesonychids, as well as large predatory birds known as phorusrhacids. The reptile groups, including crocodiles and lizards, that had survived the end-Cretaceous extinction flourished in the warm, swampy conditions, as did smaller amphibians.

Icaronycteris

The first bats, such as *Icaronycteris* (right), first appeared in the Eocene. They filled the niche left by insectivorous pterosaurs, and like them, had wings formed from membranous skin.

wings supported on all fingers

feet thought to have been webbed for swimming

Ambulocetus

As well as diversifying on the land, mammals took to the oceans. The ancestors of whales, such as *Ambulocetus* (left), evolved from piglike mammals. These primitive animals showed few adaptations to marine life.

PALEOGENE LANDMASSES

At the start of the Paleogene Period, the supercontinent of Gondwana was continuing to split up. South America was still an isolated island, and the Atlantic Ocean was becoming wider. By the end of the Eocene (see map), most of the continents were in similar positions to those they occupy today. India had begun to collide with Asia. Australia was moving north away from Antarctica but had not yet reached its present-day position.

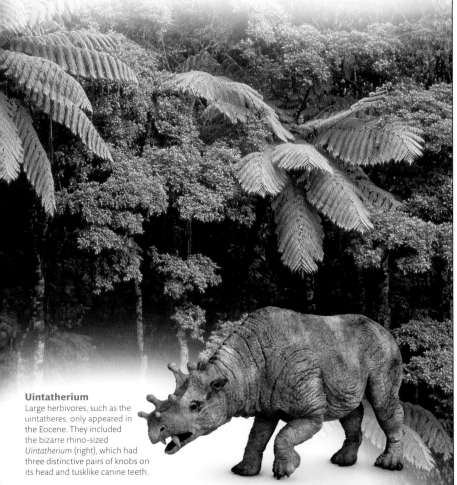

Uintatherium
Large herbivores, such as the uintatheres, only appeared in the Eocene. They included the bizarre rhino-sized *Uintatherium* (right), which had three distinctive pairs of knobs on its head and tusklike canine teeth.

| 2,000 mya | | 1,000 mya | | 500 mya | 250 mya | 0 |

MAMMALS

MAMMALS SUFFERED severe losses in the end-Cretaceous extinction, but they were able to recover rapidly. This may have been enabled by their generalized diet and small body sizes. Within a million years, they had already grown to larger sizes than throughout the entire Mesozoic, and took the top roles in ecosystems.

The balance of power shifted from the Cretaceous, and eutherians became more common than metatherians and multituberculates in most parts of the world. The major groups of placental mammals had probably originated prior to the end-Cretaceous extinction, but they radiated into many forms in the Paleocene and early Eocene. These included modern groups, such as primates, carnivorans, and rodents, alongside several groups of uncertain relationships.

By the Eocene, most of the placental groups living today had originated, and had spread into a broad array of lifestyles, including flying bats, fully aquatic whales, enormous herbivores, and fearsome carnivores. Metatherians also diversified during this time, with some becoming specialist fruit-eaters and others becoming large hypercarnivores.

Temperatures peaked early in the Eocene, leading to widespread forests, but toward the end of the Eocene they cooled, resulting in a turnover of the fauna into the Oligocene. The climate continued to become drier and cooler throughout the Oligocene, which led to the spread of grasslands. Many ungulates became adapted for running, and multituberculates went extinct after more than 130 million years on Earth.

Group: AFROTHERIA	Subgroup: Proboscidea	Time: 37–30 mya

Phiomia
FI-OHM-EE-A

This early elephant had two pairs of tusks set in very long upper and lower jaws. The tusks on the lower jaw were flattened and formed a shovel-shaped projection that was probably used to collect food or to scrape bark off trees. The tusks in the upper jaw were shorter and were probably used for fighting or for display. The upper lip was likely to have been drawn out into a short trunk. To reduce the weight of the large skull, the bones were filled with air spaces. The rest of *Phiomia*'s body was very similar to that of a modern elephant, with columnlike legs and a stocky body.

DESCRIBED BY Andrews and Beadnell 1902
HABITAT Plains and woodland

short trunk

lower "shovel-tusk" projection

Length: 16 ft (5 m)	Weight: ~3 tons (3 metric tons)	Diet: Plants

Group: PLACENTALIA	Subgroup: Afrotheria	Time: 41–27 mya

Arsinoitherium

AR-SIN-OH-IH-THEER-EE-UM

Arsinoitherium is the best-known member of the embrithopods—large, rhinolike animals that were closely related to elephants. Its most notable feature were the two huge, conical horns that jutted out from its snout. These were composed of hollow bone and may have been covered in skin. Adult animals had pointed horns, while they were rounded in juveniles.

DESCRIBED BY
Beadnell 1902

HABITAT Forests near rivers

barrel-like body

44 grinding teeth

five-toed feet

Length: 11½ ft (3.5 m)	Weight: Not calculated	Diet: Tough foliage

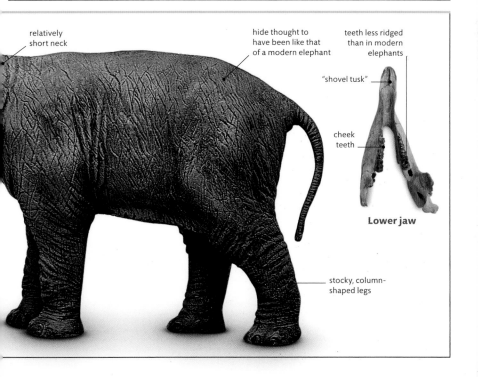

relatively short neck

hide thought to have been like that of a modern elephant

teeth less ridged than in modern elephants

"shovel tusk"

cheek teeth

Lower jaw

stocky, column-shaped legs

| Group: AFROTHERIA | Subgroup: Proboscidea | Time: 41–34 mya |

Moeritherium

MEE-RI-THEER-EE-UM

This hippolike animal, which was named after the ancient Greek name for the lake in Egypt where it was found (Moeris), is in the same group as elephants (Proboscidea). It had a low-slung, long body, with relatively short legs. Its nostrils were at the front of the skull, indicating that it did not have a trunk. The teeth were small, but two of the incisors formed small tusks. It was probably partly aquatic in its lifestyle, as is the modern hippopotamus.

DESCRIBED BY Andrews 1901
HABITAT Rivers and swamps

ears high on head

elongated, fleshy upper lip

| Length: 9¾ ft (3 m) | Weight: ~440 lb (200 kg) | Diet: Water plants |

| Group: EUARCHONTOGLIRES | Subgroup: Primates | Time: 50–46 mya |

Notharctus

NOH-THARK-TUS

This animal is one of the best-known early members of the primate order. Looking very like a modern lemur, it showed many adaptations for a life spent in trees. Its eyes faced forward, providing binocular vision for accurate judging of distances. Its legs and tail were long and strong. *Notharctus* had a type of grasping thumb that could be used for holding onto branches or food. Its fingers and toes were very long, which were also helpful for gripping. Its skull was short and its long back was very flexible.

DESCRIBED BY Leidy 1870
HABITAT Forests

eyes set well forward

short, rounded skull

long, slim body

highly flexible spine consisting of small vertebrae

hips set well back

long, grasping fingers and thumb

long legs

| Length: 16 in (40 cm) | Weight: ~10 lb (4.5 kg) | Diet: Leaves and fruit |

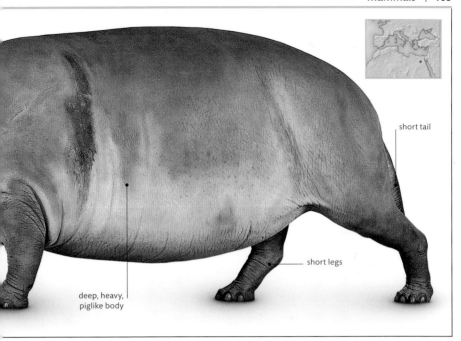

short tail

short legs

deep, heavy,
piglike body

| Group: LAURASIATHERIA | Subgroup: Chiroptera | Time: 52.5 mya |

Icaronycteris

IK-A-RON-IK-TER-IS

The oldest-known bat, *Icaronycteris* is surprisingly similar to modern forms. Analysis of its skull shows that it may have used a primitive form of echolocation. Its long tail was not joined to the legs by flaps of skin as in modern bats. The arrangement of the many teeth in the mouth indicate an insect diet. This has been confirmed by remains found in the stomach area of fossil *Icaronycteris*.

DESCRIBED BY
Jepsen 1966
HABITAT Caves

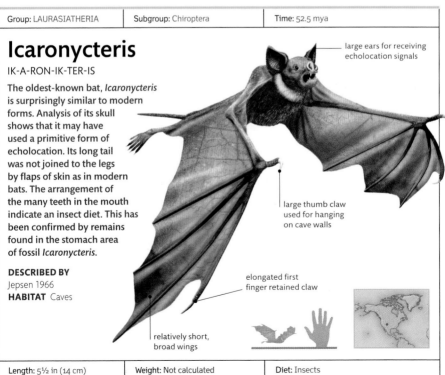

large ears for receiving echolocation signals

large thumb claw used for hanging on cave walls

elongated first finger retained claw

relatively short, broad wings

| Length: 5½ in (14 cm) | Weight: Not calculated | Diet: Insects |

Group: PLACENTALIA	Subgroup: Laurasiatheria	Time: 47–37 mya

Mesonyx

MEE-ZON-ICKS

This mesonychid carnivore, whose name means "middle claw," had a wolflike body and agile limbs that ended in five toes with small, blunt claws. The long skull had a bony crest to which the large jaw muscles were anchored. This gave a powerful bite. The canine teeth were long and sharp, and the lower molars were thin and bladelike. Paleontologists once thought that mesonychids were the ancestors of modern whales. However, based on new fossils and evidence from genetics, it is now clear that whales are more closely related to hippos.

wide mouth with powerful bite

DESCRIBED BY Cope 1871
HABITAT Shrubland, open woodland

Length: 6 ft (1.8 m)	Weight: ~45–120 lb (20–55 kg)	Diet: Meat, carrion, possibly plants

Group: LAURASIATHERIA	Subgroup: Meridiungulata	Time: 40–37 mya

Didolodus

DIE-DOH-LOH-DUS

The classification of *Didolodus* is still debated by paleontologists. Some place it with early browsing and rooting ungulates (hoofed animals), and others with a primitive litoptern (a now-extinct group of hoofed mammals). Little is known of *Didolodus*. Its teeth were very similar to those of the earliest hoofed mammals, so it may have resembled them in some respects. It was a browsing animal, with a long tail and slim legs ending in five-toed feet.

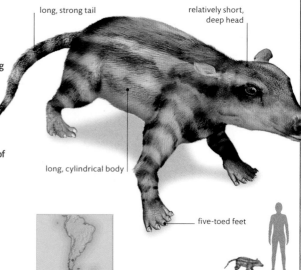

long, strong tail

relatively short, deep head

long, cylindrical body

five-toed feet

DESCRIBED BY Ameghino 1897
HABITAT Forests

Length: 24 in (60 cm)	Weight: ~33–44 lb (15–20 kg)	Diet: Leaves

Group: PLACENTALIA	Subgroup: Laurasiatheria	Time: 56–34 mya

Uintatherium

YOU-IN-TAH-THEER-EE-UM

At the time when *Uintatherium* ("Uinta beast") existed, it was one of the largest land mammals. The size of a modern rhinoceros, it was heavy limbed, with massive bones. It had three pairs of horns on its face, which varied in size. The largest horns were at the back of the head. All of them seem to have been covered in skin and possibly hair. Males appear to have had larger horns than females. It is possible that the males fought using their horns and tusklike canine teeth. The barrel-shaped body was carried on columnlike legs. *Uintatherium* walked only on its toes, which were very short, as were the other "hand" and "foot" bones. Its elephantlike feet were designed for weight-bearing and walking on dry ground. *Uintatherium* had a very small brain for its skull size compared to modern hoofed mammals.

DESCRIBED BY Leidy 1872
HABITAT Forests

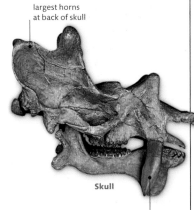

largest horns at back of skull

Skull

tusklike canine teeth, larger in males

massive, barrel-shaped body

coarse, thick hide

large, blunt horns

tusklike canines

pillarlike legs adapted for weight-bearing

Length: 11 ft (3.5 m)	Weight: ~2 tons (2 metric tons)	Diet: Leaves, fruit, water plants

Group: LAURASIATHERIA	Subgroup: Perissodactyla	Time: 59–41 mya

Phenacodus

FEN-A-COAD-US

small, short head

Phenacodus was one of the earliest ungulate (hoofed) mammals. It was relatively small and lightly built, with limbs ending in five toes. The middle toe was the largest, and the weight of the body was mainly supported on this and the two adjoining toes. These probably had short, blunt, hooflike claws. The head was small, with a proportionately small brain. The jaws held 44 teeth. The back was arched, and the tail was long and powerful. *Phenacodus* probably lived in herds, and it is possible that it was carnivorous or insectivorous, as well as herbivorous.

short-crowned upper molars

elongated middle toe bore weight

DESCRIBED BY Cope 1873
HABITAT Forests.

Length: 4 ft (1.2 m)	Weight: ~22 lb (10kg)	Diet: Leaves; possibly tubers and insects

Group: LAURASIATHERIA	Subgroup: Perissodactyla	Time: 33–23 mya

Paraceratherium

PAR-A-SER-A-THEER-EE-UM

This rhino relative was the largest land mammal known to have lived. Standing 17 ft (5.25 m) high at the shoulder, its head alone was over 4 ft (1 m) long. Hollowed-out vertebrae in the back kept the animal's weight down. The powerful legs were long and slim, and there were three toes on each foot. Despite its long legs, it is now thought unlikely that *Paraceratherium* was a fast runner. It seems to have had a flexible upper lip, allowing it to browse on leaves from trees as modern giraffes do.

probably long and flexible upper lip

DESCRIBED BY
Forster-Cooper 1911
HABITAT
Open woodland

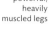

powerful, heavily muscled legs

Length: 30 ft (9 m)	Weight: ~14¾ tons (15 metric tons)	Diet: Leaves and twigs

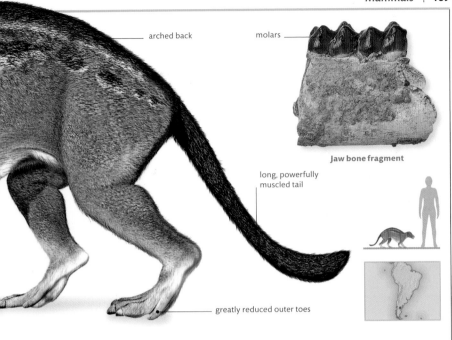

arched back

molars

Jaw bone fragment

long, powerfully
muscled tail

greatly reduced outer toes

Group: LAURASIATHERIA	Subgroup: Perissodactyla	Time: 41–27 mya

Mesohippus
ME-ZO-HIP-PUS

Mesohippus ("middle horse") had features
that seem to have been an evolutionary
response to more open environments:
its legs were longer than those of the
earlier "dawn horse" *Eohippus*, and it
had lost a toe. Of the three remaining
toes, the middle bore most of the
animal's weight. These features
increased its speed. Its teeth grew
larger, increasing their surface area
for chewing. The jaw was shallow
and the head was quite long and
pointed. The eyes were set relatively
far apart and far back on the head.

DESCRIBED BY
Marsh 1875
HABITAT
Open grassland

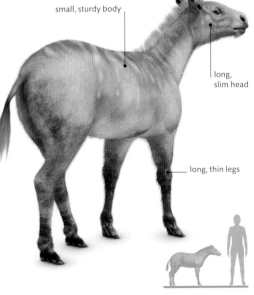

small, sturdy body

long,
slim head

long, thin legs

Length: 4 ft (1.2 m)	Weight: ~200 lb (90 kg)		Diet: Foliage

Group: CETARTIODACTYLA	Subgroup: Cetacea	Time: 48–41 mya

Ambulocetus

AM-BYU-LOH-SEE-TUS

Ambulocetus ("walking whale") is thought to be one of the most primitive cetaceans (whales). Its teeth, skull, and ear bones show features unique to this group. As its name suggests, it probably spent most of its time on land, although it may have been rather clumsy. Its feet and hands may have been webbed, and its powerful hindlimbs would have made it a strong swimmer. It is thought to have hunted by ambushing its prey in water, as modern crocodiles do.

DESCRIBED BY Thewissen et al. 1994
HABITAT Estuaries

broad, flattened tail

powerful hindlimbs

Length: 9¾ ft (3 m)	Weight: ~650 lb (295 kg)	Diet: Fish, mammals

Group: CETARTIODACTYLA	Subgroup: Cetacea	Time: 41–34 mya

Basilosaurus

BASS-IL-OH-SAW-RUS

Despite being an early whale, *Basilosaurus* ("king of the lizards") looked so much like a mythical sea monster that its bones were at first thought to be those of an ancient sea reptile. It had a flexible, whalelike body, with forelimbs shaped like paddles. It had tiny hindlimbs that may have been used in mating. *Basilosaurus* probably swam by making undulating movements of its body. Its nostrils were high on its snout, but it did not have a blowhole. It was capable of hunting large fish and other marine mammals.

DESCRIBED BY Harlan 1843
HABITAT Tropical oceans

Length: 66–82 ft (20–25 m)	Weight: ~10⅞ tons (11 metric tons)	Diet: Large fish, squid, marine mammals

poor hearing as sound was transmitted to the ear through the jaws

webbing may have been present on hands and feet

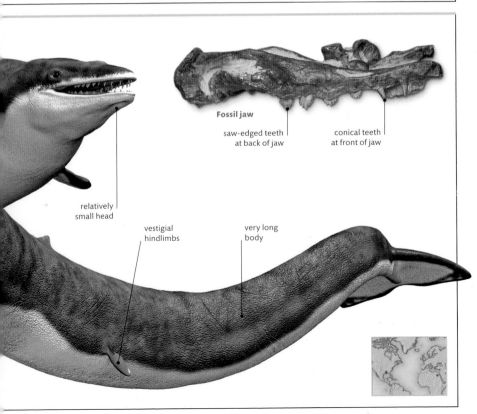

relatively small head

Fossil jaw

saw-edged teeth at back of jaw

conical teeth at front of jaw

vestigial hindlimbs

very long body

BIRDS

NEORNITHINE BIRDS survived the end-Cretaceous extinction, but the toothed enantiornithines and hesperornithids went extinct. It is debated whether any of the other archaic lineages of birds survived the extinction, but if they did, they went extinct shortly afterward. The origination of different lineages of modern birds is also uncertain, although it is clear that the major branches diverged before the end-Cretaceous extinction.

In the early Paleogene, birds diversified and started to live different lifestyles, from small, tree-dwelling birds to larger terrestrial birds, and even early penguins. In the Paleocene, ground-dwelling birds were among the largest animals on land and included herbivorous forms, such as *Gastornis* and the predatory phorusrhacids of South America.

The favorable warm climate and extensive development of forests in the early Eocene contributed to the spread and diversification of birds around the world. Late in the Eocene, the first songbirds evolved in Australia, dispersing around the world and exploding in diversity throughout the Oligocene. Meanwhile, the decline in temperature in the Oligocene led to a turnover in other species and the extinction of some lineages, such as the gastornithids. By the end of the Oligocene, songbirds were the most diverse lineage of birds, and today they still comprise 60 percent of bird species.

Group: NEOGNATHAE	Subgroup: Galloanserae	Time: 55–50 mya

Gastornis

GAS-TOR-NISS

This giant, flightless "Gaston's bird" was heavily built, with tiny wings that were incapable of flight. Its long legs were powerful and armed with clawed feet. Its head was almost the same size as that of a modern horse. *Gastornis* was earlier thought to have been a predator, but recent analysis shows that it was an herbivore and that its beak was well-adapted to eat hard fruits and seeds.

DESCRIBED BY Hébert 1855
HABITAT Forests

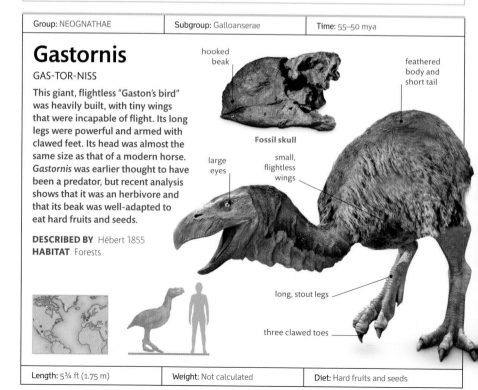

hooked beak

Fossil skull

feathered body and short tail

large eyes

small, flightless wings

long, stout legs

three clawed toes

Length: 5¾ ft (1.75 m)	Weight: Not calculated	Diet: Hard fruits and seeds

Group: NEOGNATHAE	Subgroup: Galloanserae	Time: 61–33 mya

Presbyornis
PREZ-BEE-OAR-NIS

This primitive duck was so slenderly built that paleontologists first thought it was a type of flamingo. Unlike modern ducks, *Presbyornis* had very long legs and presumably was a wader rather than a swimmer. The relative length of the neck and legs of *Presbyornis* are consistent with a wading, bottom-feeding style. Although the legs were set relatively far back, it was unlikely to have been a diving bird. Its feet were large and webbed. *Presbyornis* was highly colonial and seems to have gathered in large flocks to feed by the shores of lakes. Recent analysis of the jaw mechanism shows that it was unable to filter feed like modern ducks and was therefore a mixed feeder, similar to the magpie goose (*Anseranas semipalmata*). Hundreds of *Presbyornis* fossils have been found, representing several species that range from 1½ ft (0.5 m) to 5 ft (1.5 m) in height.

DESCRIBED BY Wetmore 1926
HABITAT Lakeshores

salt gland around edge of eye orbit

ridge along top of beak

long neck

slightly built body

long, slim wings

legs set far back

long, slim legs

large, webbed feet

Length: 1½–5 ft (0.5–1.5 m)	Weight: Not calculated	Diet: Plankton, water plants

NEOGENE PERIOD

23–2.6 MILLION YEARS AGO

THE NEOGENE (the Miocene and Pliocene Epochs) saw the continued evolution of mammals. The ice cap that had started to form at the South Pole in the Oligocene continued to expand. By the mid-Miocene, it covered all of Antarctica, further cooling the world's climate. These temperate conditions led to the development of huge expanses of grassland over Africa, Asia, Europe, and the Americas. The climate continued to cool into the Pliocene, when a large ice cap also formed at the North Pole. Most of the remaining forest areas had disappeared by the end of the Pliocene, but grasslands continued to spread.

NEOGENE LIFE

The animals of the Miocene and Pliocene were very similar to modern forms. Grasslands were filled with herds of horses, camels, elephants, and antelopes. Large carnivores hunted across the plains, and the first hominins evolved from primate ancestors. In the oceans, modern types of fish had appeared, and the primitive forms of whales had given way to more familiar, larger species.

reduced wings solely for display

sharp, hooked beak

Terrible birds

Large carnivorous birds were still some of the world's largest and most terrifying predators. The South American terror bird *Titanis* (left) hunted on open grassy plains. It moved into North America when the Panama Isthmus formed in the Pliocene.

4,600 mya	4,000 mya	3,000 mya

NEOGENE LANDMASSES

By the Neogene, the continents were nearly identical to today, including most major mountain ranges. Throughout the Triassic–Paleogene, Africa and Europe collided, forming the Alps. India's collision with Asia caused the Himalayas to rise about 40 mya. The Rocky Mountains in North America were formed during the Cretaceous–Paleocene, and the Andes in South America formed during the Triassic, uplifting throughout the Cretaceous. By the Pliocene, a land bridge linked North and South America. Australia continued to drift northward.

large canine teeth

Big cats
Many carnivores evolved large canine teeth. *Thylacosmilus* (above) was a catlike marsupial found in Miocene and Pliocene South America.

Early elephants
By the beginning of the Miocene, early elephant forms, such as the horse-sized *Phiomia* (left), were dying out and being replaced by larger forms. These, such as the shovel-tusked *Platybelodon*, would give rise to the mammoths of the Pleistocene and to modern elephant species.

2,000 mya   1,000 mya   500 mya   250 mya   0

MAMMALS

THE MAMMALS of the Miocene were a mix of archaic Paleogene lineages and early members of many modern lineages.

In Eurasia, ungulates (hoofed mammals) were common, and the perissodactyls, such as rhinoceroses, horses, and the chalicotheres, were far more diverse than today. Artiodactyls were represented by oreodonts, camels, and the omnivorous entelodonts. Early carnivorans like bears, dogs, and cats, were beginning to diversify, but the top predators, such as the saber-toothed nimravids and the "creodonts" were still archaic forms. Proboscideans, represented by the elephants today, were incredibly diverse and radiated in the Miocene as they dispersed from Africa. Whales reached a peak in diversity, and hominid apes began to evolve in Africa.

In South America, xenarthrans, such as the giant, armored glyptodonts, flourished alongside a unique group of hooved animals called meridiungulates—distant cousins of the perissodactyls. Primates and rodents, which had somehow reached South America in the Eocene by rafting across the Atlantic Ocean, diversified into their own unique forms.

The Pliocene saw the continued replacement of archaic lineages with modern ones. Toward the end of the Pliocene, North and South America became reconnected, leading to the Great American Biotic Interchange. The unique faunas mixed, resulting in extensive dispersal, restructuring of ecosystems, and many extinctions. Meanwhile, human ancestors spread out of Africa.

Group: MAMMALIA	Subgroup: Metatheria	Time: 5.3–2.6 mya

Thylacosmilus

THIGH-LA-CO-SMILE-US

Thylacosmilus was a large, carnivorous marsupial. Like the saber-tooth cats, it sported long, stabbing upper canine teeth. However, in *Thylacosmilus*, these teeth grew continuously throughout life, and there were no incisor teeth in the lower jaw. Bony guards in the lower jaw protected the teeth when the jaws were closed. The neck and shoulders were strong and heavily muscled, which allowed for the teeth to be pulled back to disembowel carcasses. The anatomy of *Thylacosmilus* shows that it was not an active predator, but was most likely a scavenger that specialized in eating the internal organs of carrion.

DESCRIBED BY Riggs 1933
HABITAT Plains

large, deep skull

stabbing saber teeth

Length: 4 ft (1.2 m)	Weight: ~250 lb (115 kg)	Diet: Slow-moving, hoofed mammals

Group: MAMMALIA	Subgroup: Metatheria	Time: 18–16 mya

Cladosictis

CLAD-OH-SICK-TIS

This carnivorous marsupial species was short lived. Some paleontologists have suggested that it may have had an otterlike lifestyle—hunting fish in rivers—but it may also have eaten the eggs and young of land-living creatures. *Cladosictis* had a long, lightly built body; short limbs; and a doglike skull. Its tail was long and thin. The teeth were similar to those of carnivorous placental mammals: there were sharp incisors at the front of the jaw, with pointed canines and shearing molars behind them.

DESCRIBED BY
Ameghino 1887
HABITAT Woodland

long body and thick neck

doglike snout

Length: 2½ ft (80 cm)	Weight: ~8–18 lb (3.5–8 kg)	Diet: Small animals, possibly fish and eggs

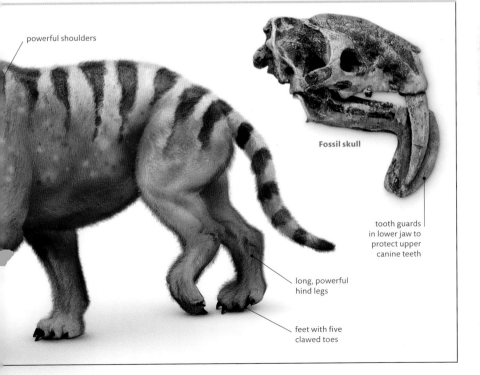

powerful shoulders

Fossil skull

tooth guards in lower jaw to protect upper canine teeth

long, powerful hind legs

feet with five clawed toes

Group: AFROTHERIA	Subgroup: Proboscidea	Time: 18–4 mya

Gomphotherium

GOM-FO-THEER-EE-UM

Gomphotherium had a pair of upper jaw tusks for fighting and display and long lower jaws that formed a food "shovel." It had a trunk as long as the lower tusks to help with feeding. Later species had fewer teeth, with more pronounced ridges for grinding.

DESCRIBED BY
Burmeister 1837
HABITAT Grassland, marsh, forest

thick hide

curved tusks

ridged surface for efficient grinding

Cheek teeth

Length: 16 ft (5 m)	Weight: ~4½–7½ tons (4–7 metric tons)	Diet: Plants

Group: AFROTHERIA	Subgroup: Proboscidea	Time: 16–11 mya

Platybelodon

PLAT-EE-BEL-OH-DON

The shovel arrangement of the lower tusks in this family of elephants reached extreme proportions in *Platybelodon*. The flattened lower tusks were very broad, with an indentation near the top for the upper pair of tusks to slot into while the mouth was closed. The cheek teeth were flat, and there were sharper teeth at the front of the jaw. The trunk was very wide. *Platybelodon* seems to have used its shovel-tusks to scoop up water weeds and other soft plants. The tail was relatively long. As a highly specialized feeder, it was vulnerable to environmental change and was a short-lived genus.

DESCRIBED BY Borissiak 1928
HABITAT Wet prairies

larger ears than more primitive elephants

large head

Length: 20 ft (6 m)	Weight: ~4½–5½ tons (4–5 metric tons)	Diet: Soft water plants

Group: LAURASIATHERIA	Subgroup: Carnivora	Time: 20–2.6 mya

Amphicyon

AM-FIE-SIGH-ON

The amphicyonids were a family of "bear-dogs," of which *Amphicyon* ("ambiguous dog") was a typical member. A powerful predator, it had well-muscled shoulders, a heavily built body, and strong legs. It may have lived a lifestyle similar to that of modern bears.

DESCRIBED BY
Lartet 1836
HABITAT Plains

powerful shoulders

wolflike teeth

strong, heavy feet armed with sharp claws

Length: 8 ft (2.5 m)	Weight: ~1,300 lb (600 kg)	Diet: Mostly mammals, some plants

Group: CARNIVORA	Subgroup: Canidae	Time: 32–25 mya

Cynodesmus

SY-NOH-DES-MUS

An early member of the dog family, *Cynodesmus* was a coyote-sized animal with a short snout and a long body. Its legs were similar to those of modern dogs but were not as efficient for running. The feet had clawed toes, with the claws being partially retractable.

DESCRIBED BY
Scott 1893
HABITAT Plains

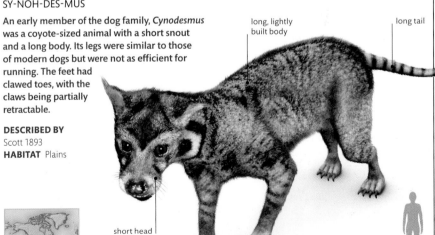

long, lightly built body

long tail

short head and snout

Length: 3½ ft (1 m)	Weight: ~155 lb (70 kg)	Diet: Smaller mammals, carrion

Group: LAURASIATHERIA	Subgroup: Carnivora	Time: 37–20 mya

Hoplophoneus

HOP-LOE-FOE-NE-US

Hoplophoneus, a member of a family of "false saber-tooth cats," first arose in Europe, then gradually spread into North America. It was a large and powerful hunting cat with a long, low body and relatively short legs. Its head and snout were short, with forward-facing eyes that probably allowed binocular vision and therefore accurate judgment of distances—an important attribute for a hunter. Its upper canine teeth were elongated into thick, stabbing "saber" teeth, just as in the true saber-tooth cats. These teeth were thick and curved and extended far below the level of the lower jaw, which was capable of opening to an angle of 90 degrees, enabling it to use these teeth to stab its prey. In comparison, the lower canines were very small.

DESCRIBED BY Cope 1874
HABITAT Plains

long, heavy tail

relatively short yet powerful legs

Length: 8 ft (2.5 m)	Weight: ~350 lb (160 kg)	Diet: Mammals

Group: LAURASIATHERIA	Subgroup: Perissodactyla	Time: 20–5 mya

Teleoceras

TELL-EE-OH-SEA-RAS

This mammal was a member of the rhinoceros family. It had a long body, extremely short legs, and a small conical nose horn. It is now thought that *Teleoceras* was a terrestrial grazer much like a modern rhinoceros. A large number of *Teleoceras* remains have been found in Ashfall Fossil Beds, Nebraska. The animals died due to inhaling volcanic ash that buried their waterhole.

DESCRIBED BY
Hatcher 1894
HABITAT
Grasslands

low, barrel-shaped body held capacious gut

short neck

very short but sturdy legs

long cheek teeth

Length: 13 ft (4 m)	Weight: ~3 tons (3 metric tons)	Diet: Brush, grass

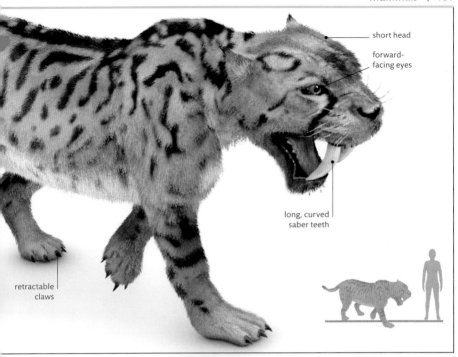

short head

forward-facing eyes

long, curved saber teeth

retractable claws

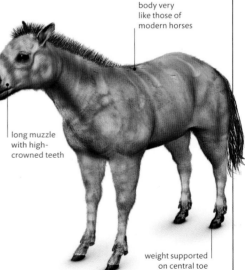

Group: LAURASIATHERIA	Subgroup: Perissodactyla	Time: 16–5 mya

Merychippus

MER-EE-CHIP-PUS

Merychippus ("ruminant horse") was the first horse to feed exclusively on grass and the first one to have a head similar to that of modern horses. The muzzle was longer than in earlier horses, the jaw deeper, and the eyes farther apart. Its neck was also longer than in earlier horses, as it spent much of its time grazing. The middle toe on each foot had developed into a hoof that did not have a pad on the bottom. In some species, the outer two toes only touched the ground when running; in others, they were larger.

body very like those of modern horses

long muzzle with high-crowned teeth

DESCRIBED BY Leidy 1856
HABITAT Grassy plains

weight supported on central toe

Length: 6½ ft (2 m)	Weight: ~440 lb (200 kg)	Diet: Grass

| Group: LAURASIATHERIA | Subgroup: Perissodactyla | Time: 13–2.5 mya |

Hipparion

HIP-PAIR-EE-ON

Hipparion ("better horse") was one of several groups of grazing three-toed primitive horses that lived in the Miocene. It was a lightly built animal that greatly resembled a modern pony, with a long jaw and slim legs. The horse's full weight was borne on the enlarged central toe, which had developed a recognizable hoof. The two outer toes were very reduced in size and did not reach the ground. A tendon in the foot increased the springiness of the gait, giving the advantage of greater speeds. The teeth were large and high-crowned for grazing. *Hipparion* was a very successful genus of early horse, spreading over the world in large herds for millions of years.

DESCRIBED BY de Christol 1832
HABITAT Plains

Upper jaw bone

large premolars

high-crowned molars with many cusps

large eyes set far back along skull

bony pocket (antorbital fossa) larger in males

long, squarish muzzle with large nostrils

moderately long tail

very slim, light legs

elongated foot bone

large central toe forming a hoof

Bones of hind foot

| Length: 5 ft (1.5 m) | Weight: ~250 lb (115 kg) | Diet: Grass |

Group: CETARTIODACTYLA	Subgroup: Cetacea	Time: 23–15 mya

Eurhinodelphis

UOU-RHINE-OH-DEL-FIS

Eurhinodelphis ("true-nose dolphin") was one of the most common dolphins in the Miocene. Its most distinctive feature was its long snout, which may have been used to strike at its prey. The structure of the ear had become more complex than in earlier toothed whales, indicating that *Eurhinodelphis* had developed some form of echolocation system. The skull was slightly asymmetrical, as in modern toothed whales, with a blowhole at the top of the head.

asymmetrical skull

elongated snout

DESCRIBED BY
Du Bus 1867
HABITAT
Oceans

hydrofoil-shaped flippers

powerful, double-lobed tail

Length: 12 ft (3.7 m)	Weight: Not calculated	Diet: Fish

Group: CETARTIODACTYLA	Subgroup: Cetacea	Time: 14–7 mya

Cetotherium

SET-OH-THEER-EE-UM

Resembling a small version of the modern rorquals, *Cetotherium* was an early baleen whale, with baleen plates instead of teeth. The inside of the baleen was edged with coarse hairs that filtered krill, plankton, and small fish. *Cetotherium*'s baleen plates were probably quite short. It lacked echolocation. Its head was symmetrical, and it probably had two blowholes.

long, streamlined body like modern baleen whales

DESCRIBED BY
Brandt 1843
HABITAT
Oceans

short baleen plates

elongated, wide head

Length: 13 ft (4 m)	Weight: ~2 tons (2 metric tons)	Diet: Plankton

BIRDS

THE SMALL SIZE and delicate skeleton of birds mean that their fossils are much less common than those of other animals. Nevertheless, several sites around the world with exceptional preservation show that a great diversity of birds had evolved by the Neogene, including a vast array of seafaring birds. Many of these, such as penguins, cormorants, and boobies, are still alive today. Others left no descendants, such as the enormous *Osteodontornis* (see p.186), which had a fearsome beak adorned with toothlike bony projections.

Throughout the Neogene, many bird lineages became larger, most likely associated with cooling climates. This trend resulted in some of the largest birds to ever live, such as *Argentavis* (see p.186). Many flightless birds also became larger, including not only ratites such as ostriches, emus, and moa, but also ground-dwelling parrots and penguins.

By the Miocene, terrestrial bird ecosystems were structured very much like those of today. Ducks, owls, hawks, fowl, and parrots had all evolved and diversified, alongside the incredibly species-rich songbirds. By the end of the Pliocene, all of the modern orders of birds had evolved, including several genera that survive today. Some of these orders have no fossil records, but modern techniques using DNA show that they must have diverged by this time.

Phorusrhacids remained top predators in South America, and they were highly successful in the grasslands promoted by the cool, arid climates of the Miocene and Pliocene. However, they would go extinct shortly after the Great American Biotic Interchange, most likely due to competition from an influx of mammalian predators.

Group: NEOAVES	Subgroup: Phorusrhacidae	Time: 18–16 mya

Phorusrhacos

FOR-US-RAKE-US

Phorusrhacos was one of the dominant land predators in South America at the time it existed. It had very strong legs, capable of running at high speed; stubby, flightless wings; a long neck; and a proportionately large head. This ended in a huge, hooked beak that could have torn through flesh easily or have stabbed into prey. The lower jaw was smaller than the upper jaw. There were three toes on each of the feet, all of which were armed with sharp claws.

DESCRIBED BY Ameghino 1887
HABITAT Plains

short skull

large upper mandible

hooked beak

Length: 5 ft (1.5 m)	Weight: ~176 lb (80 kg)		Diet: Small mammals, carrion

Group: NEOAVES	Subgroup: Phorusrhacidae	Time: 5–1.8 mya

Titanis

TIE-TAN-IS

Titanis ("terror crane") was aptly named. This giant flightless bird was one of the most efficient predators of its time in North America. Its head was as large as that of a modern horse, and it had a huge, curved beak. Although it had no teeth, the sharp hook at the end of the beak was very efficient at tearing through flesh. It had highly reduced wings that were ineffective for hunting or flight. *Titanis* had a long neck, and males may have had an ornamental crest on the top of the head. It had long, agile legs and three-toed feet with long talons. It could undoubtedly run at high speeds when hunting.

DESCRIBED BY Brodkorb 1963
HABITAT Grassy plains

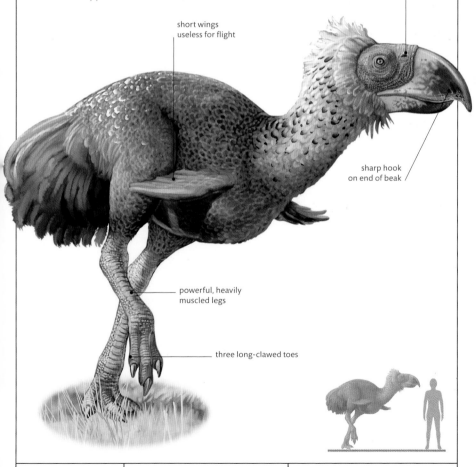

nostrils high on top of beak

short wings useless for flight

sharp hook on end of beak

powerful, heavily muscled legs

three long-clawed toes

Length: 8 ft (2.5 m)	Weight: ~330 lb (150 kg)	Diet: Mammals

Group: GALLOANSERAE	Subgroup: Pelagornithidae	Time: 16–5 mya

Osteodontornis

OS-TEE-OH-DON-TOR-NIS

One of the largest birds ever to have flown, *Osteodontornis* was a bony-toothed seabird. It had a large, heavy body and long, narrow wings designed for gliding long distances. The neck had a natural S-shaped curve, meaning that the head was held over the shoulders in flight. The beak was stout and rounded, with toothlike bony projections edging each jawbone.

DESCRIBED BY Howard 1957
HABITAT Seashores

Length: 4 ft (1.2 m)	Weight: Not calculated	Diet: Fish

Group: NEORNITHES	Subgroup: Teratornithidae	Time: 9–6.8 mya

head possibly
bald with neck
fringe of feathers

Argentavis

AR-GEN-TAH-VIS

Only a few bones of this large bird of prey have been discovered, but these indicate a wingspan of over 23 ft (7 m), which is twice the size of that of the largest living bird, the wandering albatross. In appearance, it was probably similar to a modern vulture, and it may have been a scavenger. Its beak was large and hooked and was used to grasp prey, because its clawed feet were not well adapted for this. *Argentavis* used its vast wings to soar effortlessly, riding the warm thermals of air.

deep, hooked
beak

large eyes

DESCRIBED BY Campbell and Tonni 1980
HABITAT Inland and mountainous areas

Height: 5 ft (1.5 m)	Weight: ~175 lb (80 kg)	Diet: Carrion, large herbivorous mammals

pelicanlike head

rounded bill
with small
hook at end

large wingspan of
up to 20 ft (6 m)

wing feathers
up to 5 ft
(1.5 m) long

long wings compared
to body size

large feet with
three forward-
facing, clawed toes

QUATERNARY PERIOD

2.6 MILLION YEARS AGO–PRESENT

THE QUATERNARY PERIOD includes the Pleistocene and Holocene Epochs. The Pleistocene was a time when the world was in the grip of a great ice age, with enormous ice sheets covering most of the northern hemisphere. Glaciers also formed in the high mountain regions of the world, including the Andes and the Himalayas. Over the next one and a half million years, the Earth passed through at least four ice ages. Between ice ages, the climate was warmer. The most recent ice age ended about 10,000 years ago, at the beginning of the Holocene, and saw mass extinctions of mammal species.

QUATERNARY LIFE

Animals responded to the colder conditions of the Pleistocene by migrating toward equatorial regions (for example, lizards) or evolving furry coats (for example, mammoths and the woolly rhino, Coelodonta). Truly modern humans, Homo sapiens, evolved during the Pleistocene, along with other, less successful human species, such as Homo neanderthalensis.

large canine teeth

powerful hindlimbs

Canine carnivores

Many species of dog lived during the Pleistocene. Aenocyon dirus (left) was very like a modern wolf but heavier. It survived into the Holocene. Fossil remains show that dire wolves and saber-tooth cats often fought over territory and food.

4,600 mya	4,000 mya	3,000 mya

QUATERNARY LANDMASSES

During the Pleistocene Epoch, huge ice sheets covered most of North America, Europe, and northern Asia. There were land bridges from North America to Eastern Asia and between Australia and New Guinea. At the start of the Holocene, rising sea levels caused by melting ice sheets covered these land bridges. Africa and Australia continued to move northward to occupy their present positions (see map).

Litopterns

The Pleistocene grasslands of South America were home to herds of strange, hoofed animals called litopterns. These, such as the camel-sized *Macrauchenia* (right), were grazing animals, adapted for life on open plains.

Giant marsupials

Herds of giant, grazing marsupials in Australia, such as *Diprotodon* (left), became rarer as the climate grew drier with the continent's continuing drift northward. They survived into the Holocene but may have been hunted to extinction by humans.

| 2,000 mya | 1,000 mya | 500 mya | 250 mya | 0 |

MAMMALS

BY THE QUATERNARY, mammal ecosystems were essentially modern. Carnivorans took over the roles of top predators, and the first big cats evolved, including *Smilodon* (see p.194). Perissodactyls had declined in diversity, possibly because of competition with ruminant artiodactyls, like deer, bovids, and giraffes, which have a more efficient digestive system. Many of these ungulates, including horses, camels, and rhinos, had ranges across the northern hemisphere. Some groups of proboscideans had gone extinct, but elephants remained successful throughout Eurasia as well as North America.

The Pleistocene ice ages had a profound impact on mammals. The spread of ice caps and glaciers forced mammal populations to move farther south, and made vast swaths of land uninhabitable. Many groups of mammals became much larger and developed thick fur coats to insulate them against the freezing temperatures.

Humans continued to spread across Asia and Europe, and multiple species coexisted at the same time. The ability of these species to use tools meant that they had a profound impact on mammal populations, and there was a severe decline in the numbers of most large mammals.

At the end of the Pleistocene, there was selective extinction of many of the large-bodied mammals. Many lineages went entirely extinct, but some were able to survive in smaller parts of their ranges, resulting in the distributions we see today. It is clear that both climate change and human hunting were involved in these extinctions, as many coincided with the arrival of humans.

Group: CARNIVORA	Subgroup: Canidae	Time: 125,000–9,500 ya

Aenocyon dirus

AY-NO-SY-ON DIE-RUS

This extinct member of the dog family, whose name means "dire wolf," was a larger and heavier version of the modern wolf. It had a wider head, stronger jaws, and longer teeth than modern members of the dog family. It had long, powerful legs, and its toes had blunt claws that could not be retracted. It was probably both a scavenger and an active hunter.

DESCRIBED BY (Leidy 1858)
HABITAT Grassland and woodland

large, erect ears

thick, wiry coat

powerful haunches

five-toed feet with blunt claws

Length: 6½ ft (2 m)	Weight: ~115 lb (53 kg)	Diet: Mammals, carrion, possibly fruit

Group: AFROTHERIA	Subgroup: Proboscidea	Time: 1.5 mya–10,000 ya

Mammuthus columbi

MAM-UT-US KO-LUM-BE

The largest of all mammoth species, the Columbian mammoth was probably the largest terrestrial animal alive during the last ice age. Unlike the woolly mammoth, this mammoth was well-adapted to the warmer climates it lived in and did not have such thick fur. Besides its immense size, its most distinguishing feature was its tusks. These curled backward evenly and were up to 15 ft (4.8 m) long. They could weigh up to 185 lb (84 kg).

DESCRIBED BY (Falconer 1857)
HABITAT Plains

fatty hump
behind head

back sloping
down from
shoulders
to hips

short hair over
the whole body

long,
thick tusks

thick, flexible trunk

elephantine legs

Length: 15 ft (4.5 m)	Weight: ~8–10 tons (8–10 metric tons)	Diet: Grass, leaves, flowering plants

| Group: AFROTHERIA | Subgroup: Proboscidea | Time: 700,000–4,000 ya |

Mammuthus primigenius

MAM-UT-US PRIM-EE-GEN-EE-US

Mammuthus primigenius, the woolly mammoth, was relatively small for a mammoth. It was adapted to living in the cold climates of northern tundras, with a thick coat of long, dark hair overlaying a downy undercoat. The hair would have been light brown, to brown to black, depending on the individual. A thick layer of fat under the skin helped with insulation, and there was also a fatty hump behind the head used for food storage. Its ears were smaller than those of modern elephants, helping reduce heat loss. The long, curved tusks appear to have been used to scrape away ice from the ground when feeding, as well as for protection and in dominance rituals. The woolly mammoth survived until relatively recent times, and paleontologists are therefore very familiar with its anatomy and appearance. Several well-preserved specimens have been found frozen in the permafrost of Siberia and Alaska, and cave paintings by early humans depict it clearly.

ridges for grinding tough plant material

Upper cheek tooth

DESCRIBED BY (Blumenbach 1799)
HABITAT Frozen tundra

long, curved tusks

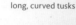

small, rounded ears

short tail

Frozen remains of a young mammoth

| Length: 11½ ft (3.5 m) | Weight: ~6.6 tons (6 metric tons) | Diet: Low-lying tundra vegetation |

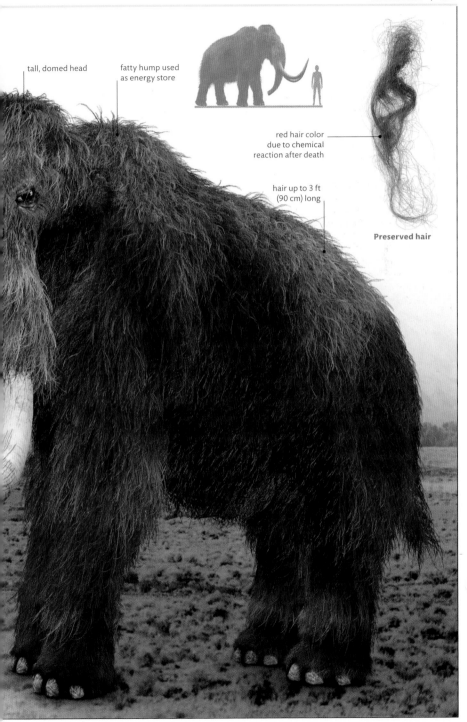

tall, domed head

fatty hump used as energy store

red hair color due to chemical reaction after death

hair up to 3 ft (90 cm) long

Preserved hair

Group: CARNIVORA	Subgroup: Felidae	Time: 2.5 mya–10,000 ya

Smilodon

SMILE-OH-DON

Smilodon was the cat popularly thought of as a saber-tooth tiger. Its sharp canine teeth were huge and were serrated along their rear edges to increase their cutting ability. They were also oval in cross-section. This meant that they were strong while presenting minimum resistance when biting. Such long teeth meant that the cat's jaw had to open to an angle of more than 120 degrees to allow the teeth to be driven into its prey. However, it seems the teeth may have broken easily if they came into contact with bone. *Smilodon* therefore probably hunted by biting through an animal's neck. *Smilodon*'s arms and shoulders were very powerful in order to produce a strong downward motion of the head. *Smilodon* appears to have hunted in packs, probably preying on large, slow, thick-skinned animals.

DESCRIBED BY Lund 1842
HABITAT Grassy plains

FOSSIL SKULL

Smilodon is very well known. Over 2,000 individuals have been excavated from the Rancho La Brea tar pits, a famous prehistoric predator trap, in Los Angeles, California.

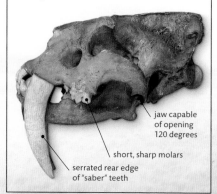

jaw capable of opening 120 degrees

short, sharp molars

serrated rear edge of "saber" teeth

Length: 5–8¼ ft (1.5–2.5 m)	Weight: ~710 lb (320 kg)	Diet: Large mammals

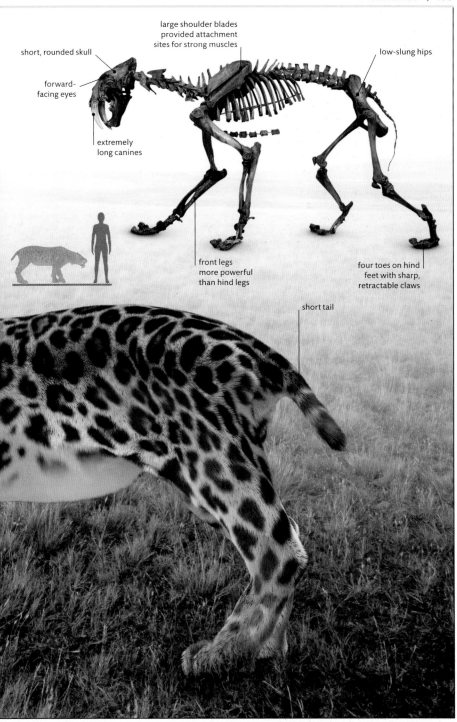

short, rounded skull

forward-facing eyes

large shoulder blades provided attachment sites for strong muscles

low-slung hips

extremely long canines

front legs more powerful than hind legs

four toes on hind feet with sharp, retractable claws

short tail

Group: CARNIVORA	Subgroup: Felidae	Time: 5–1 mya

Dinofelis

DIE-NOH-FEEL-IS

Dinofelis ("terrible cat") was a panther-sized cat. It had flattened canine teeth that were intermediate in length between those of the saber-tooth cats and those of biting cats, such as lions. It was probably an agile climber with long, strong legs and sharp, retractable claws. Its tail was long and flexible and could be used to aid balance. The skull of *Dinofelis* was short, and its eyes were forward-facing and positioned for binocular vision—essential for judging distances accurately when hunting or leaping. Its coat is likely to have had a pattern of camouflage similar to those of modern forest-dwelling cats.

DESCRIBED BY
Zdansky 1924
HABITAT Dense forest

dappled coat for camouflage

flat head with forward-facing eyes

retractable claws remained sharp

long canine teeth

Length: 7 ft (2.2 m)	Weight: ~350 lb (160 kg)	Diet: Mammals

Group: CARNIVORA	Subgroup: Felidae	Time: 1 mya to present

Panthera

PAN-THAIR-A

There were several lionlike species of *Panthera* that are now extinct. *Panthera spelaea*, the European cave lion, was the largest cat ever to have lived. It is often seen in cave paintings. *Panthera atrox* lived in North America. Both species killed prey by biting the neck with their canine teeth, and they had sharp claws that could be retracted under a flap of skin.

sharp cutting edges

strong jaw bone **Lower jaw**

DESCRIBED BY Oken 1816
HABITAT Grassland

Length: 11 ft (3.5 m)	Weight: ~520 lb (235 kg)	Diet: Meat

Group: LAURASIATHERIA	Subgroup: Meridiungulata	Time: 9 mya–10,000 ya

Macrauchenia
MAK-RAW-CHEN-EE-A

This curious animal (whose name means "great llama") had a number of camel-like features, such as its size, its small head, and its long neck. However, its three-toed feet were more like those of a rhinoceros. Challenging the conventional interpretation of a tapirlike proboscis, it is now suggested that *Macrauchenia* had a nose similar to that of a modern moose. It had long, slim legs, and the flexibility and strength of the ankles suggest it was a relatively agile animal. The high-crowned cheek teeth indicate that *Macrauchenia* may have been a browser and a grazing animal.

camel-like body shape

long toe bone

Right forefoot bones

DESCRIBED BY
Owen 1838
HABITAT Woodland

Length: 10 ft (3 m)	Weight: ~1,540 lb (700 kg)	Diet: Plants

Group: LAURASIATHERIA	Subgroup: Perissodactyla	Time: 3.7 mya–10,000 ya

Coelodonta
SEEL-OH-DON-TA

The woolly rhinoceros, *Coelodonta* ("hollow tooth"), evolved to withstand cold conditions. Its fur was thick and shaggy, its body was massive with short legs, and its ears were small. It had a huge pair of horns on its snout, the front one of which grew to over 3¼ ft (1 m) in length in older males.

thick, shaggy, gray-brown fur

small ears to reduce heat loss

long horn made of keratin

DESCRIBED BY
Bronn 1831
HABITAT Tundra

Length: 11 ft (3.5 m)	Weight: ~3–4 tons (3–4 metric tons)	Diet: Plants

BIRDS

THE INSTABILITY OF THE climate during the transition from the Neogene to the Quaternary had a profound impact on birds. Several lineages went extinct during the glaciation of the Pleistocene, including many of the larger-bodied birds that had been successful during the Neogene. *Titanis* (see p.185), the last surviving phorusrhacid, was able to spread as far north as Texas during the Great American Biotic Interchange. However, it went extinct early in the Pleistocene, ending the reign of large, flightless avian predators.

Some large-bodied birds survived on isolated islands, including New Zealand and Madagascar, where they had no natural predators. However, as humans spread across the world and began to disperse to these islands, they found these birds to be easy prey. A great number of these species were hunted to extinction, including famous examples like the Dodo, the elephant bird, *Vorombe titan* (see p.199), and the moa, *Dinornis* (see below). Human arrival often introduced invasive predators, such as cats, dogs, and snakes, so island birds have continued to decline at alarming rates.

Habitat fragmentation caused by both glaciation and humans has disproportionately impacted birds of all sizes worldwide, but studies show that conservation efforts can help to slow their decline.

Group: NEORNITHES	Subgroup: Palaeognathae	Time: 40,000–600 ya

Dinornis

DIE-NOR-NIS

This was the tallest flightless bird ever to have existed and was one of a dozen types of moas that survived in New Zealand until modern times. It was a slow-moving bird, with a bulky body; long, heavily built legs; and a long neck. Preserved feathers show that its plumage was mostly gray and fluffy. Its beak was short and sharp-edged and was used to shear at vegetation. Gizzard stones were used to help digest plant material. The numbers of *Dinornis* declined rapidly after the arrival of humans in New Zealand about 10,000 years ago, and they were hunted to extinction around 600 years ago.

DESCRIBED BY (Owen 1843)
HABITAT River areas, bushland

short beak

long neck

heavy, wingless body

long, heavily built legs

three-toed feet with short claws

Length: 11½ ft (3.5 m)	Weight: ~880 lb (400 kg)	Diet: Twigs, seeds, fruit

Group: NEORNITHES	Subgroup: Palaeognathae	Time: 10,000–1,000 ya

Vorombe titan

VUH-ROM-BAY TIE-TAN

Vorombe titan, commonly called the "elephant bird of Madagascar," was the heaviest bird species known to have existed. It was a wingless bird, with long, thick legs and feet ending in three widely spread toes. The thickness of the thigh bone indicates that *Vorombe* was generally a slow-moving bird and could probably not run at high speeds. The small head had a toothless beak, and the only protection against predators was the bird's size and strength. Several eggs have been found fossilized in the mud of swampy areas near rivers.

DESCRIBED BY
(Andrews 1894)
HABITAT Forests

small head

toothless beak

long neck

Vorombe egg

feathered, wingless body

ankle joint

elongated, thick thighs

three widely spaced toes with small claws

toe articulations

Metatarsus (foot bone)

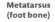

Length: up to 10 ft (3 m)	Weight: ~1,400 lb (650 kg)	Diet: Seeds, fruit

ADDITIONAL DINOSAURS

This section consists of a brief description of almost 300 dinosaurs not included in the main body of the book. The entries are arranged alphabetically and each includes, wherever possible, its geological period and the country in which the principal fossil finds were made.

Abrictosaurus
A small, early ornithopod dinosaur. Jurassic. South Africa.

Achelousaurus
A ceratopsian that appears to be an intermediate form between *Einiosaurus* and *Pachyrhinosaurus*. Late Cretaceous. USA.

Acheroraptor
A dromaeosaurid that lived alongside *Tyrannosaurus rex* and *Triceratops*. Late Cretaceous. USA.

Achillobator
A large deinonychosaur with a sicklelike claw on each foot. Late Cretaceous. Mongolia.

Acrocanthosaurus
An *Allosaurus*-like theropod with spines on the back supporting a sail or ridge. Early Cretaceous. USA.

Acrotholus
The earliest known pachycephalosaur. Late Cretaceous. Canada.

Adasaurus
A lightly built dromaeosaur with long, sickle-shaped claws on each hind foot. Late Cretaceous. Mongolia.

Aegyptosaurus
A sauropod known only from isolated bones. Late Cretaceous. North Africa.

Aeolosaurus
A large sauropod. Late Cretaceous. Argentina.

Afrovenator
A theropod. Cretaceous. Africa.

Agilisaurus
A lightly built, herbivorous dinosaur. Middle Jurassic. China.

Alamosaurus
The last known sauropod and North America's only known titanosaur. Late Cretaceous. USA.

Albertavenator
A troodontid dinosaur. Late Cretaceous. Canada.

Albertosaurus
A *Tyrannosaurus*-like theropod. Late Cretaceous. North America.

Alectrosaurus
A large theropod. Late Cretaceous. China and Mongolia.

Algoasaurus
A small sauropod. Early Cretaceous. South Africa.

Alocodon
A small, thyreophoran dinosaur known only from teeth. Late Jurassic. Portugal.

Altirhinus
An iguanodontid with a beak on its snout and a spiked thumb on each hand. Early Cretaceous. Mongolia.

Altispinax
A theropod with long spines along its back. Early Cretaceous. England.

Alvarezsaurus
A small, lightly built theropod with an extremely long, thin, flat tail. Part of the Alvarezsauria, with *Shuvuuia*. Late Cretaceous. Argentina.

Alwalkeria
An early Saurischian. Late Triassic. India.

Alxasaurus
A large, primitive therizinosaur. Cretaceous. Mongolia.

Amargasaurus
A sauropod with unusually long spines running along its back. Early Cretaceous. Argentina.

Ammosaurus
A sauropod with large hands and thumb claws. Now considered the same as *Anchisaurus*. Early Jurassic. USA.

Ampelosaurus
A large, titanosaurid sauropod dinosaur. Late Cretaceous. France.

Amtosaurus
Possibly an ankylosaur, but identity and classification are doubtful. Late Cretaceous. Mongolia.

Amurosaurus
A hadrosaur similar to *Lambeosaurus*. Not yet formally described. Cretaceous. Russia.

Amygdalodon
A large sauropod. Late Jurassic. Southern Argentina.

Anasazisaurus
A hadrosaur known only from a skull. Late Cretaceous. USA.

Anchiceratops
A long-frilled ceratopsian. Late Cretaceous. Canada.

Anchiornis
A well-known, birdlike paravian. Late Jurassic. China.

Andesaurus
An enormous titanosaurid sauropod. Cretaceous. Argentina.

Anserimimus
An *Ornithomimus*-like dinosaur. Late Cretaceous. Mongolia.

Antarctosaurus
A very large, heavily built sauropod. Late Cretaceous. South America, India, and Russia.

Anzu
A large, toothless caenagnathid with a tall crest on its head. Late Cretaceous. USA.

Apatoraptor
A caenagnathid, known from a relatively complete articulated skeleton. Late Cretaceous. Canada.

Aquilops
A primitive neoceratopsian ornithischian. Early Cretaceous. USA.

Aragosaurus
A huge sauropod. Early Cretaceous. Spain.

Aralosaurus
A hadrosaur ornithopod known only from a skull. Late Cretaceous. Kazakhstan.

Archaeornithoides
A theropod with unserrated teeth. Late Cretaceous. Mongolia.

Archaeornithomimus
An *Ornithomimus*-like dinosaur with primitive clawed fingers. Late Cretaceous. North America and China.

Argyrosaurus
A large sauropod. Late Cretaceous. South America.

Arkansaurus
A theropod, possibly an ornithomimid. Late Cretaceous. USA.

Arrhinoceratops
A horned ceratopsian with a short nose horn. Late Cretaceous. Canada.

Arstanosaurus
A hadrosaur with a flat head. Late Cretaceous. Kazakhstan.

Asfaltovenator
A primitive tetanuran that shows that Carnosauria is a natural group. Middle Jurassic. Argentina.

Asiaceratops
Primitive ceratopsian. Fragmentary remains only. Late Cretaceous. Russia.

Atlascopcosaurus
An iguanodont. Early Cretaceous. Australia.

Aublysodon
Small *Tyrannosaurus*-like theropod with smooth teeth. Late Cretaceous. North America.

Aucasaurus
An abelisaur dinosaur known from a complete skeleton. Late Cretaceous. Argentina.

Auroraceratops
A small, primitive ceratopsian. Early Cretaceous. China.

Austrosaurus
A primitive sauropod dinosaur. Cretaceous. Australia.

Avaceratops
A small ceratopsian dinosaur, possibly a juvenile. Late Cretaceous. USA.

Avimimus
An *Oviraptor*-like theropod. May have had feathered wings. Late Cretaceous. Mongolia and China.

Bactrosaurus
A duck-billed ornithopod with a flat head and high-spined vertebrae. Late Cretaceous. China and Uzbekistan.

Bagaceratops
A very small ceratopsian. Late Cretaceous. Mongolia.

Bagaraatan
A primitive theropod. Now considered a tyrannosaur. Late Cretaceous. Mongolia.

Bahariasaurus
A tetanuran theropod. Full classification uncertain. Late Cretaceous. Egypt and Niger.

Balaur
An unusual paravian theropod with two sickle claws on each foot. Late Cretaceous. Romania.

Bambiraptor
A juvenile theropod with a sickle-shaped claw on the second toe. Originally thought to be a juvenile *Velociraptor* or *Saurornitholestes*. Late Cretaceous. USA.

Barsboldia
A large duck-billed ornithopod. Late Cretaceous. Mongolia.

Beibeilong
A giant caenagnathid known only from embryos and a nest of eggs. Late Cretaceous. China.

Beipiaosaurus
A herbivorous theropod with primitive feathers. Now known to be a therizinosaur. Cretaceous. China.

Bellusaurus
A small sauropod. May be young of another genus. Jurassic. China.

Bilkanosaurus
Bulky sauropodomorph. Late Triassic. South Africa and Lesotho.

Borealopelta
An exquisitely preserved ankylosaur, complete with skin and scales. Early Cretaceous. Canada.

Borogovia
A *Troodon*-like theropod with a sickle-shaped claw on each foot. Late Cretaceous. Mongolia.

Brachyceratops
A ceratopsian with a nose horn and two brow horns. Late Cretaceous. USA.

Brachylophosaurus
Primitive hadrosaurid ornithopod with a flat crest on the top of its head. Late Cretaceous. North America.

Breviceratops
A ceratopsian. Late Cretaceous. Mongolia.

Brontosaurus
Originally thought to be the same as *Apatosaurus*. It is now recognized as a valid but separate animal. Late Jurassic. USA.

Buriolestes
An early, carnivorous sauropodomorph. Late Triassic. Brazil.

Byronosaurus
A *Troodon*-like theropod. The first of its family with unserrated teeth. Late Cretaceous. Mongolia.

Caenagnathus
A lightly built caenagnathid oviraptorosaur. Late Cretaceous. North America.

Callovosaurus
An ornithopod. Mid-Jurassic. England.

Camelotia
A large sauropodomorph. Late Triassic. England.

Carcharodontosaurus
A large carnosaur. Cretaceous. Africa.

Cathetosaurus
A sauropod known only from scant fossils. May be the same as *Camarasaurus*. Late Jurassic. USA.

Cedarosaurus
A *Brachiosaurus*-like sauropod. Late Cretaceous. USA.

Cetiosauriscus
A sauropod. Jurassic. England.

Changmiania
A primitive ornithopod known from two skeletons in sleeping poses. Early Cretaceous. China.

Chaoyangosaurus
A small, bipedal ornithischian, probably a pachycephalosaur. Late Jurassic. China.

Chilantaisaurus
A large *Allosaurus*-like carnosaur. Late Cretaceous. China and Russia.

Chilesaurus
An unusual herbivorous dinosaur that is either an early branching ornithischian or a theropod. Late Jurassic. Chile.

Chindesaurus
A lightly built theropod. One of the earliest known dinosaurs. Late Triassic. North America.

Chirostenotes
Along with *Caenagnathus*, now known to be a caenagnathid oviraptorosaur. Late Cretaceous. Canada.

Chubutisaurus
An unusual sauropod with heavily hollowed vertebrae. Late Cretaceous. Argentina.

Chungkingosaurus
A stegosaurid. Late Jurassic. China.

Claosaurus
A primitive hadrosaur. Late Cretaceous. USA.

Coloradisaurus
A massospondylid sauropodomorph. Late Triassic. Argentina.

Concavenator
An unusual carcharodontid theropod with a hump on its back. Early Cretaceous. Spain.

Conchoraptor
A small oviraptorid theropod. Late Cretaceous. Mongolia.

Corythoraptor
An ornately crested oviraptorid theropod. Late Cretaceous. China.

Cryolophosaurus
A theropod. Early Jurassic. Antarctica.

Dacentrurus
An early stegosaurid with two rows of asymmetrical plates along its back and large spines along its tail. Late Jurassic. England, France, Portugal, and Spain.

Daspletosaurus
A heavily built tyrannosaurid theropod with brow horns. Late Cretaceous. Canada.

Datousaurus
A *Cetiosaurus*-like sauropod with a long neck and a very solid skull. Mid-Jurassic. China.

Deltadromeus
A long-limbed and fast-running tetanuran theropod. Late Cretaceous. Morocco.

Dicraeosaurus
A diplodocid sauropod with a long neck and a whiplike tail. Jurassic. Tanzania.

Dilong
A small, primitive, crested tyrannosauroid with feathers. Early Cretaceous. China.

Draconyx
An *Iguanodon*-like dinosaur. Late Jurassic. Portugal.

Dracopelta
A nodosaur. Late Jurassic. Portugal.

Dromiceiomimus
An *Ornithmimus*-like dinosaur. Cretaceous. Canada.

Dryptosaurus
The first theropod to be discovered in North America. Late Cretaceous. USA.

Echinodon
A small, early ornithischian. Late Jurassic. England.

Einiosaurus
A ceratopsian. Late Cretaceous. USA.

Elaphrosaurus
A lightly built theropod. Previously classed as an ornithomimid; now considered a noasaurid, a subgroup within Abelisauria. Cretaceous. Tanzania.

Elmisaurus
A theropod known from hands and feet. Now known to be a caenagnathid oviraptorosaur, with *Caenagnathus* and *Chirostenotes*. Late Cretaceous. Mongolia.

Emausaurus
An ornithischian with skin covered with cone-shaped and flat armor plates. Jurassic. Germany.

Enigmosaurus
A large therizinosaur. Cretaceous. Mongolia.

Eoceratops
A primitive ceratopsian with a short frill and three short facial horns. Late Cretaceous. North America.

Eolambia
An early hadrosaurlike ornithopod. Cretaceous. USA.

Eotyrannus
A theropod. Cretaceous. England.

Epachthosaurus
A very large armored sauropod. Cretaceous. Argentina.

Erectopus
An allosauroid. Cretaceous. France and Egypt.

Erlikosaurus
A large therizinosaur. Late Cretaceous. Mongolia.

Euhelopus
A large sauropod with a very long neck and bulky body. Jurassic. China.

Euronychodon
A tetanuran theropod. Cretaceous. Portugal and Uzbekistan.

Euskelosaurus
A large sauropodomorph. Early Jurassic. Lesotho, South Africa, and Zimbabwe.

Eustreptospondylus
A large tetanuran theropod with a primitive hip structure. Jurassic. England.

Falcarius
A primitive therizinosaur known from a bonebed with thousands of bones. Early Cretaceous. USA.

Garudimimus
An *Ornithomimus*-like dinosaur. Cretaceous. Mongolia.

Gasparinisaura
A very small ornithopod, probably a juvenile. Cretaceous. Argentina.

Genyodectes
A large theropod. Cretaceous. Argentina.

Gigantoraptor
The largest oviraptorosaur, rivaling *Tyrannosaurus rex* in size. Late Cretaceous. China.

Gilmoreosaurus
A primitive ornithischian hadrosaur. Cretaceous. China.

Gobihadros
An exceptionally preserved basal hadrosauroid. Late Cretaceous. Mongolia.

Gobivenator
A beautifully preserved troodontid. Late Cretaceous. Mongolia.

Gongbusaurus
An ornithischian. Jurassic. China.

Gorgosaurus
A tyrannosaurid, once thought to be *Albertosaurus*. Cretaceous. North America.

Goyocephale
A pachycephalosaur with a thick skull, flat head, knobs and spikes on the skull, and large teeth. Cretaceous. Mongolia.

Gryposaurus
A hadrosaurid. Cretaceous. Canada.

Guanlong
A primitive, crested tyrannosauroid. Late Jurassic. China.

Halszkaraptor
A swanlike, semiaquatic dromaeosaur. Late Cretaceous. Mongolia.

Haplocanthosaurus
A sauropod. Late Jurassic. USA.

Haplocheirus
A primitive alvarezsaur, linking them to theropods and revealing the pattern of forelimb reduction. Late Jurassic. China.

Harpymimus
A primitive ornithomimosaur. Early Cretaceous. Mongolia.

Hesperosaurus
A primitive stegosaurid with a single row of rounded plates along its back. Originally called *Hesperisaurus*. Jurassic. USA.

Histriasaurus
A large sauropod that may have had a sail along the back. Early Cretaceous. Croatia.

Homalocephale
A pachycephalosaur with a flat skull bordered by bony knobs. Late Cretaceous. Mongolia.

Hoplitosaurus
An ankylosaur. Early Cretaceous. USA.

Hulsanpes
A small theropod known from foot bones and part of the braincase. Late Cretaceous. Mongolia

Hypacrosaurus
A large hadrosaur. Cretaceous. North America.

Hypselosaurus
A small titanosaurid sauropod whose eggs were the first dinosaur eggs discovered. Late Cretaceous. France and Spain.

Kamuysaurus
A hadrosaur known from a complete skeleton. Late Cretaceous. Japan.

Kritosaurus
A hadrosaurid. Late Cretaceous. Argentina.

Labocania
A tetanuran theropod. Late Cretaceous. Mexico.

Laplatasaurus
An armored sauropod that had a very long neck with grooved vertebrae. Late Cretaceous. Argentina and Uruguay.

Leaellynasaura
A small hypsilophodontid with large eyes. Early Cretaceous. Australia.

Ledumahadi
A large sauropod showing the evolution of large size before columnar legs. Early Jurassic. South Africa.

Leptoceratops
A primitive ceratopsian from Cretaceous. North America.

Limusaurus
An unusual ceratosaur that became toothless over its lifetime. Late Jurassic. China.

Lophorhothon
A hadrosaurid. Cretaceous. USA.

Losillasaurus
An enormous diplodocid sauropod. Jurassic and Cretaceous. Spain.

Lycorhinus
An early ornithopod. Jurassic. South Africa.

Magyarosaurus
A small titanosaurid sauropod. Late Cretaceous. Romania.

Majungasaurus
A large theropod with a small horn over the eyes. Late Cretaceous. Madagascar.

Malawisaurus
A sauropod. Early Cretaceous. Malawi.

Marshosaurus
A large theropod. Late Jurassic. USA.

Masiakasaurus
A theropod. Now considered a noasaurid, along with *Elaphrosaurus*. Cretaceous. Madagascar.

Megaraptor
A theropod. Cretaceous. Argentina.

Mei
A small troodontid theropod known from two skeletons in sleeping poses. Early Cretaceous. China.

Melanorosaurus
A large sauropod. Late Triassic and Early Jurassic. Lesotho and South Africa.

Metriacanthosaurus
A theropod with high dorsal spines. Cretaceous. England.

Micropachycephalosaurus
A tiny ceratopsian—one of the smallest dinosaurs known. Late Cretaceous. China.

Microvenator
The earliest caenagnathid oviraptorosaur. Early Cretaceous. China and USA.

Moros
A small, primitive tyrannosauroid. Late Cretaceous. USA.

Mussaurus
A *Plateosaurus*-like sauropodomorph known from 20-ft (6-m) long adults and remains of hatchlings—the smallest dinosaur skeletons yet discovered. Triassic. Argentina.

Muttaburrasaurus
An *Iguanodon*-like ornithopod. Early Cretaceous. Australia.

Mymoorapelta
An ankylosaurid. Cretaceous. Australia.

Naashoibitosaurus
A hadrosaur known only from a skull. May be a species of *Kritosaurus*. Cretaceous. USA.

Nanosaurus
A small ornithischian. Jurassic. North America.

Nanyangosaurus
An ornithopod dinosaur. Cretaceous. China.

Nedcolbertia
A small theropod known from three partial skeletons. Probably an ornithomimid. Early Cretaceous. USA.

Nemegtosaurus
A sauropod known from a skull, vertebrae, and hindlimb bones. Late Cretaceous. Mongolia and China.

Neovenator
An *Allosaurus*-like theropod, with a puffinlike skull profile. Early Cretaceous. England.

Neuquenraptor
A theropod with a sickle claw on each foot. Late Cretaceous. Argentina.

Nigersaurus
A primitive rebbachisaurid sauropod. Early Cretaceous. Niger.

Nipponosaurus
A small hadrosaur with a bony head crest. Cretaceous. Russia.

Noasaurus
A small theropod. Cretaceous. Argentina.

Notatesseraeraptor
An early theropod similar to coelophysids and dilophosaurids. Late Triassic. Switzerland.

Nothronychus
The first therizinosaur found outside Asia. It may have been feathered. Cretaceous. USA.

Nqwebasaurus
An ornithomimid with a very large claw on the first finger. Cretaceous. South Africa.

Nyasasaurus
Probably the first dinosaur. Triassic. East Africa.

Ohmdenosaurus
A sauropod known from one complete shin bone. Early Jurassic. Germany.

Oksoko
An unusual two-fingered oviraptorid known from a group of four individuals preserved resting together. Late Cretaceous. Mongolia.

Omeisaurus
A large *Cetiosaurus*-like sauropod with a very long neck. Jurassic. China.

Opisthocoelicaudia
A large, short-tailed titanosaur, probably the same dinosaur as *Nemegtosaurus*. Cretaceous. Mongolia.

Orodromeus
An ornithopod found with unhatched eggs and young. Its young are thought to have been able to fend for themselves after hatching. Late Cretaceous. USA.

Ozraptor
An abelisauroid theropod with three-fingered hands and a stiff tail. Jurassic. Australia.

Pachyrhinosaurus
A short-frilled ceratopsian that may have had a snout horn. Cretaceous. North America.

Panoplosaurus
A nodosaurid ankylosaur with no tail club. Cretaceous. North America.

Paranthodon
A stegosaur known from a jaw bone with teeth. Cretaceous. South Africa.

Parksosaurus
An ornithopod. Cretaceous. North America.

Patagonykus
An alvarezsaur, alongside *Alvarezsaurus* and *Shuvuuia*. Late Cretaceous. Argentina.

Patagosaurus
A primitive *Cetiosaurus*-like sauropod. Mid-Jurassic. Argentina.

Pawpawsaurus
A large nodosaur with armor over most of its body but no tail club. Cretaceous. USA.

Pelecanimimus
The first ornithomimosaur discovered in Europe. It had about 220 teeth, more than any other known theropod, and fossil remains show evidence of feathers. Cretaceous. Spain.

Pelorosaurus
A sauropod known from incomplete skeletons and fossilized skin impressions. Early Cretaceous. England and France.

Phyllodon
A small *Hypsilophodon*-like dinosaur. Jurassic. Portugal.

Pinacosaurus
An ankylosaur. Cretaceous. Mongolia.

Pisanosaurus
Possibly an early ornithischian known only from fragmentary fossils. Its classification is debated. Late Triassic. Argentina.

Piveteausaurus
A megalosauroid, possibly 26 ft (11 m) in length. Jurassic. France.

Planicoxa
An ornithopod. Cretaceous. USA.

Poekilopleuron
A *Megalosaurus*-like theropod. Jurassic. France.

Polacanthus
A primitive ankylosaur with spines. Cretaceous. England.

Prenocephale
A *Stegoceras*-like pachycephalosaur. Cretaceous. Mongolia.

Probactrosaurus
An *Iguanodon*-like ornithopod dinosaur. Early Cretaceous. China.

Proceratosaurus
A crested theropod. Now known to be an early tyrannosaur. Jurassic. England.

Prosaurolophus
A hadrosaur. Late Cretaceous. North America.

Protarchaeopteryx
A birdlike, nonflying theropod with feathers on the arms, most of the body, and the short tail. Early Cretaceous. China.

Protohadros
The oldest-known iguanodontian. Late Cretaceous. USA.

Pyroraptor
A *Deinonychus*-like dinosaur. May be the same as *Variraptor*. Cretaceous. France.

Qantassaurus
A kangaroo-sized ornithopod. Cretaceous. Australia.

Quaesitosaurus
Large titanosaur known only from a partial skull. Cretaceous. Mongolia.

Quilmesaurus
A medium-sized theropod. Late Cretaceous. Argentina.

Rahonavis
A dinosaur or primitive bird with sickle-shaped toe claws and a long, bony tail. Late Cretaceous. Madagascar.

Rapetosaurus
A *Titanosaurus*-like sauropod. Late Cretaceous. Madagascar.

Rebbachisaurus
A rebbachisaurid sauropod dinosaur that may have had a sail on its back. Cretaceous. Morocco and Niger.

Regaliceratops
An unusual ceratopsian with a highly ornamented, crownlike frill. Late Cretaceous. Canada.

Rhabdodon
An *Iguanodon*-like ornithopod. Late Cretaceous. Austria, France, Romania, and Spain.

Rhoetosaurus
A *Cetiosaurus*-like sauropod. Mid-Jurassic. Australia.

Ricardoestesia
A small theropod. Cretaceous. North America.

Riojasaurus
A heavily built sauropodomorph. Late Triassic and Early Jurassic. Argentina.

Ruehleia
A recently discovered primitive *Plateosaurus*-like sauropodomorph. Triassic. Germany.

Saichania
An ankylosaur with a clubbed tail and bony spikes and knobs running along its sides. Both body armor and belly armor have been found. Cretaceous. Mongolia.

Santanaraptor
A theropod known from partial skeleton and skin impressions. Early Cretaceous. Brazil.

Sarcolestes
An early nodosaur or ankylosaur known only from a partial lower jaw. Jurassic. England.

Sauroposeidon
A *Brachiosaurus*-like sauropod. Cretaceous. USA.

Saurornitholestes
A *Velociraptor*-like theropod. Cretaceous. Canada.

Scipionyx
A theropod known from a single hatchling that includes soft tissues. Now considered a compsognathid. Cretaceous. USA.

Secernosaurus
A hadrosaur—the first to be found in South America. Cretaceous. Argentina.

Segisaurus
A goose-sized, birdlike theropod whose collarbone was similar in structure to that of true birds. Jurassic. USA.

Segnosaurus
Now known to be a therizinosaur. Cretaceous. Mongolia.

Shamosaurus
An ankylosaur. Cretaceous. Mongolia.

Shantungosaurus
The largest-known hadrosaur. Late Cretaceous. China.

Siamosaurus
A large, sail-backed, *Spinosaurus*-like theropod. Cretaceous. Thailand.

Siamotyrannus
A theropod now included within Metriacanthosauridae. Cretaceous. Thailand.

Silvisaurus
A nodosaur with a relatively long neck and spines jutting out from the back and possibly the tail. Cretaceous. USA.

Sinornithosaurus
A dromaeosaurid. The fossil had traces of downy fibers on its skin. Jurassic. China.

Spiclypeus
A ceratopsian with a highly ornamented frill. Late Cretaceous. USA.

Stenopelix
A ceratopsian, possibly similar to *Psittacosaurus*, known from hip and leg bones. Early Cretaceous. Germany.

Stokesosaurus
A theropod that may have been the earliest tyrannosauroid. Jurassic. USA.

Struthiosaurus
An ankylosaur. Late Cretaceous. Europe.

Supersaurus
A diplodocid sauropod. One of the longest dinosaurs yet discovered. Late Jurassic. USA.

Suskityrannus
A small, primitive tyrannosauroid. Late Cretaceous. USA.

Talarurus
An ankylosaur. Cretaceous. Mongolia.

Tangvayosaurus
A titanosaurid sauropod. Cretaceous. Asia.

Tarchia
An ankylosaur with a very large tail club and large braincase. Cretaceous. Mongolia.

Tawa
An early theropod known from complete skeletons and skulls. Late Triassic. USA.

Telmatosaurus
A hadrosaur. Cretaceous. France, Romania, and Spain.

Tendaguria
A sauropod. Jurassic. Tanzania.

Tenontosaurus
A large ornithopod with relatively long arms. Cretaceous. North America.

Thanatotheristes
A tyrannosaurid closely related to *Daspletosaurus*. Late Cretaceous. Canada.

Thescelosaurus
An ornithopod dinosaur. Cretaceous. North America.

Timimus
A theropod known from leg bones. Cretaceous. Australia.

Timurlengia
A small, early tyrannosauroid with an advanced, tyrannosauridlike brain. Late Cretaceous. Uzbekistan.

Torvosaurus
A large theropod. Late Jurassic. USA.

Tsintaosaurus
A hadrosaur with a bony crest on the head. Cretaceous. China.

Tylocephale
A small pachycephalosaur known only from incomplete skull. Cretaceous. Mongolia.

Unenlagia
A birdlike theropod. Now known to be a member of dromaeosauridae. Cretaceous. Argentina.

Utahraptor
A large dromaeosaurid. Cretaceous. USA.

Valdoraptor
A tetanuran theropod known from footbones. Early Cretaceous. England.

Variraptor
A dromaeosaurid theropod. Late Cretaceous. France.

Venenosaurus
A titanosaurid sauropod. Cretaceous. USA.

Vespersaurus
A desert-dwelling noasaurid with an unusual, reduced foot. Late Cretaceous. Brazil.

Wannanosaurus
A tiny, primitive pachycephalosaur. Cretaceous. China.

Wendiceratops
An ornate ceratopsian with a highly decorated frill and three horns on the face. Late Cretaceous. Canada.

Wuerhosaurus
A stegosaur with smaller plates than *Stegosaurus*. Early Cretaceous. Mongolia.

Xenotarsosaurus
A theropod known from a few vertebrae and hind-leg bones. Cretaceous. Argentina.

Xiaosaurus
A small ornithischian. Jurassic. China.

Xuanhuaceratops
An ornithischian. Cretaceous. China.

Yandusaurus
Ornithopod ornithischian. Jurassic. China.

Yaverlandia
An early maniraptoran. Cretaceous. England.

Yi
A small, unusual dinosaur with batlike wings formed of skin rather than feathers. Late Jurassic. China.

Yunnanosaurus
A large sauropodomorph—the only sauropodomorph known with self-sharpening, chisel-shaped teeth. Jurassic. China.

Zephyrosaurus
A *Hypsilophodon*-like dinosaur known from a partial skull and vertebrae. Cretaceous. USA.

Zizhongosaurus
A primitive sauropod. Jurassic. China.

Zuniceratops
An early ceratopsian with brow horns. Cretaceous. USA.

GLOSSARY

This glossary is an easy-reference guide to the technical terms that are used in this book. It focuses mainly on the terms used to describe different groups of dinosaurs and other forms of prehistoric life. It also includes scientific names used to describe anatomical features. If you cannot find the term you are looking for here, check the general index; the information you need may be found elsewhere in the book. Words in bold type within the entries have their own glossary entries.

■ Acanthodians
The earliest jawed **vertebrates**. Primitive fish, also known as spiny sharks, that lived from the Ordovician to the Carboniferous.

■ Acetabulum
The hip socket.

■ Aerofoil
The curved surface of a wing that aids flight by creating an upward force.

■ Aetosaurs
A group of early Archosauromorph that superficially resembled crocodiles, with bulky bodies and leaf-shaped teeth.

■ Agnathans
"Jawless fish"—primitive **vertebrates** that flourished in Early Paleozoic times.

■ Algae
Primitive plants and plantlike organisms.

■ Allosaurs
Large, fairly primitive **tetanuran** (stiff-tailed) **theropods**.

■ Ammonites
Extinct, predatory marine **invertebrates (cephalopods)**. These animals had a shell (usually spiral-coiled) containing air-filled chambers; the animal lived only in the outer chamber.

■ Amniotes
Animals whose eggs contain an amnion, a membrane that surrounds the embryo. Mammals, birds, and **reptiles** are amniotes.

■ Amphibians
Vertebrates whose young live in the water (breathing through gills), but usually live on land as adults (breathing with lungs). Living amphibians include newts, salamanders, frogs, and toads.

■ Angiosperms
Flowering plants, which produce seeds enclosed in fruit (an ovary).

■ Ankylosaurs
A family of heavily armored, plant-eating, **quadrupedal ornithischian dinosaurs** that lived from the mid-Jurassic to the Late Cretaceous Periods.

■ Arboreal
An organism that spends most of its life in trees, off the ground.

■ Archosaurs
A major group of **reptiles** that includes the **crocodilians**, **pterosaurs**, **dinosaurs**, and **aves** (birds).

■ Arthropods
A group of **invertebrates** with **exoskeletons** made of chitin, segmented bodies, and jointed limbs. Insects, spiders and scorpions, **trilobites**, and **crustaceans** are members of this group.

■ Artiodactyls
Ungulates (hoofed mammals) with an even number of toes. Pigs, camels, deer, giraffes, and cattle are modern animals in this group.

■ Aves
The scientific name for birds.

■ Baltica
An ancient continent of the Paleozoic Era.

■ Bipedal
Walking on the hindlimbs rather than on all four legs. See also **Quadrupedal**.

■ Bivalves
Aquatic **molluscs** enclosed by a two-part, hinged shell.

■ Brachiopods
Marine **invertebrates** with two joined valved shells.

■ Brachiosaurids
A group of huge **sauropods** with spoon-shaped teeth and long forelimbs. They lived in the Late Jurassic and Early Cretaceous Periods.

■ Braincase
The bones of the skull that contain and protect the brain.

■ Brontotheres
Also known as titanotheres. An extinct family of large, rhinoceroslike mammals.

■ Browser
An animal that eats tall foliage (leaves, trees, or shrubs).

■ Camarasaurids
A group of relatively short-necked **sauropods** of the Jurassic and Cretaceous Periods.

■ Carinates
A group of birds with deep-keeled breastbones.

■ Carnivora
A group of sharp-toothed, meat-eating mammals, including cats and dogs.

■ Carnosaurs
A group of large **theropods** that lived during the Jurassic and Cretaceous Periods.

■ **Centrosaurines**
A group of rhinoceroslike **ceratopsian dinosaurs**—most had long horns on the snout and a short neck frill.

■ **Cephalopods**
Molluscs with tentacles surrounding a large head. These soft-bodied **invertebrates** include squid, octopuses, cuttlefish, and **ammonites**.

■ **Cerapods**
A group of **ornithischian dinosaurs** that included the **ornithopods** and the **marginocephalians**.

■ **Ceratopsians**
A group of plant-eating **ornithischian dinosaurs** with beaks and bony head frills along the back of the skull.

■ **Ceratosaurs**
A major group of **theropod dinosaurs**—those in which the three hip bones (**ilium, ischium,** and **pubis**) are fused.

■ **Cetaceans**
Marine mammals with a streamlined body and flippers for limbs. The group includes whales and dolphins.

■ **Choristoderes**
A group of crocodilelike **diapsid reptiles**.

■ **Clade**
A grouping of animals (or other organisms) that share anatomical features derived from the same ancestor.

■ **Coelurosaurs**
A group of **tetanuran theropods** that includes the **maniraptorans, ornithomimids,** and **tyrannosaurids**.

■ **Condylarths**
A group of herbivorous mammals that arose in the Paleogene. Some had clawed feet; others had blunt hooves. This group is not natural, but is used as a descriptive grade for **ungulate**-like (hoofed) mammals whose relationships are not known.

■ **Confuciornithids**
A family of early birds similar to *Confuciornis*.

■ **Creodonts**
A group of meat-eating mammals with clawed feet, a small brain, large jaws, and many sharp teeth that were the dominant carnivorous mammals during the end of the Paleogene. Although this group is not natural, it is used as a descriptive grade for carnivorelike mammals whose relationships are not known.

■ **Crocodilians**
A group of **archosaurs** that includes alligators, crocodiles, and gharials. They evolved during the Late Triassic Period.

■ **Crinoids**
Plant-shaped **echinoderms** (sea lilies).

■ **Crustaceans**
A class of **invertebrates** with a hard **exoskeleton**, jointed legs, and a bilaterally symmetrical segmented body.

■ **Cryogenian Period**
A geological time period that lasted from 720 to 635 million years ago.

■ **Cycads**
Primitive seed plants that dominated Jurassic habitats. They are palmlike trees, with separate male and female plants.

■ **Cynodonts**
A group of herbivorous and carnivorous **synapsids** that appeared late in the Permian Period. Mammals originated within this group.

■ **Deinonychosaurs**
A group of advanced **theropod dinosaurs** with a long, sharp, sickle-shaped claw on the second toe of each hind foot. This group includes **dromaeosaurs** and **troodontids**.

■ **Diapsids**
A **clade** of animals, distinguished by two temporal **fenestrae**, that includes **archosaurs** and **lepidosaurs**.

■ **Dicynodonts**
Piglike, herbivorous **therapsids** with two large tusks in the upper jaw.

■ **Dimorphism**
Having two forms, for example, sexual dimorphism between males and females of the same species.

■ **Dinocephalians**
Late Permian **therapsids**. Some were meat-eating; others were plant-eating or omnivores.

■ **Dinosaurs**
A **clade** of **reptiles**, partly distinguished by a largely to fully open **acetabulum** and erect limbs. They were wholly terrestrial. Only one major group of dinosaurs, **aves** (birds), survived after the end of the Cretaceous.

■ **Diplodocids**
A family of huge **sauropods** characterized by a small head with peglike teeth and nostrils opening at the top of the head.

■ **Docodonts**
A group of primitive mammals.

■ **Dromaeosaurids**
A family of small, fast **theropods**, with large, retractable, sickle-shaped toe claws and large eyes.

■ **Echinoderms**
Saltwater **invertebrates** whose living members have five arms or divisions of the body (or multiples of five).

■ **Ectotherms**
Animals, often called "cold blooded," whose internal temperature changes with the surrounding environment.

■ **Elasmosaurs**
A family of long-necked **plesiosaurs**.

■ **Enantiornithes**
A group of toothless birds that lived during the Cretaceous. Their shoulder blade (scapula) and coracoid (a small bone connected to the scapula) are oriented in the opposite way of that of modern birds.

■ **Endotherms**
Animals, often called "warm blooded," that maintain a relatively constant internal temperature by generating their own body heat.

■ **Euornithes**
This group encompasses all modern birds. It also includes some extinct forms that left no descendants.

■ **Eurasia**
The continent formed by the combined land masses of Europe and Asia.

■ **Evolution**
The theoretical process by which the gene pool of a population changes in response to environmental pressures, natural selection, and genetic mutations.

■ **Exoskeleton**
A tough, outer body covering made of chitin (a type of protein) or calcium carbonate.

■ **Family**
A group of related or similar organisms. A family contains one or more **genera**.

■ **Femur**
The thigh bone.

■ **Fenestra (pl. fenestrae)**
A natural, windowlike hole or opening in a bone. The skull has many fenestrae.

■ **Fibula**
The smaller of the two bones of the lower leg.

■ **Fossil**
Any direct evidence of ancient life, including preserved remains, chemical traces, or behavioral traces.

■ **Furcula**
The "wishbone" in birds.

■ **Gastralia**
Thin ribs in the belly area not attached to the backbone.

■ **Gastropods**
A class of **molluscs** with a suckerlike foot and often a spiral shell.

■ **Genus (pl. genera)**
A group of related or similar organisms. A genus contains one or more **species**. A group of similar genera comprise a **family**.

■ **Gondwana**
The southern supercontinent formed after the breakup of the supercontinent **Pangaea**. It included present-day South America, Africa, India, Australia, and Antarctica.

■ **Gracile**
Small and slender. Some species have both gracile and **robust** forms, possibly representing differences between males and females.

■ **Graptolite**
Extinct, tiny marine colonial animals, with a soft body and a hard outer covering.

■ **Grazer**
An animal that eats low-lying vegetation, such as grasses.

■ **Gymnosperms**
Seed-bearing plants that do not produce flowers.

■ **Hadrosaurs**
A group of "duck-billed" Cretaceous **quadrupedal ornithopods**.

■ **Herbivore**
An animal that eats plants.

■ **Hesperornithes**
A family of early birds similar to *Hesperornis*.

■ **Homeothermic**
An animal that keeps a fairly constant body temperature.

■ **Horsetail**
A primitive, spore-bearing plant with rhizomes that was common during the Paleozoic and Mesozoic Eras.

■ **Hypsilphodontids**
A group of small, herbivorous **ornithopod ornithischians** that were widespread in the Jurassic and Cretaceous Periods.

■ **Iapetus Ocean**
The precursor of the Atlantic Ocean, between the ancient continents of **Laurentia** and **Baltica**.

■ **Ichthyornithes**
A family of early birds similar to *Ichthyornis*.

■ **Iguanodontids**
A group of herbivorous **ornithopod ornithischians** that were widespread in the Cretaceous Period.

■ **Ilium**
One of the three (paired) bones of the pelvis.

■ **Insectivore**
An organism (animal or plant) that eats insects.

■ **Invertebrates**
Animals without a backbone.

■ **Ischium**
One of the three (paired) bones of the pelvis.

■ **Juvenile**
A young or immature individual.

■ **K-Pg Extinction**
The mass extinction that occurred at the boundary of the Cretaceous and the end of the Paleogene.

■ **Lagomorphs**
A group of mammals that

became widespread during the end of the Paleogene and includes modern rabbits and hares.

■ **Lagosuchians**
A group of early **archosaurs** that were probably ancestors of the **dinosaurs**.

■ **Laurasia**
The northern supercontinent formed after the breakup of **Pangaea**.

■ **Laurentia**
An ancient continent of the Paleozoic Era.

■ **Lepidosaurs**
The group of **reptiles** that includes snakes and lizards.

■ **Lepospondyls**
Small, extinct **amphibians** that resembled salamanders or snakes. They lived through the Carboniferous and Permian Periods.

■ **Litopterns**
A group of extinct hoofed mammals that resembled camels and horses.

■ **Lobe-finned fish**
A group of fish whose fins are supported on fleshy lobes. Lobe-finned fish, or **Sarcopterygians**, appeared during the Silurian Period.

■ **Lycopods**
A group of **lycopsid** plants, also known as club mosses. They were at their peak in the Carboniferous Period.

■ **Lycopsids**
Primitive **vascular plants** that evolved during the Devonian Period.

■ **Maniraptorans**
A group of advanced **theropods** with birdlike characteristics. It included **dromaeosaurs**, **oviraptorids**, **troodontids**, **therizinosaurs**, and **aves**.

■ **Marginocephalians**
A group of **ornithischian** dinosaurs with a bony frill or shelf on the back of the skull. This group includes the **ceratopsians** and **pachycephalosaurs**.

■ **Marsupials**
Mammals, including modern-day kangaroos, that give birth to small, undeveloped young that grow and mature in a pouch on the mother's abdomen.

■ **Mastodons**
An extinct group of mammals closely related to elephants.

■ **Megalosaurs**
A group of large **theropods**, less advanced than **allosaurs**.

■ **Mesosaurs**
Extinct, lizardlike aquatic **reptiles**.

■ **Molluscs**
A group of **invertebrates** including **gastropods** and **cephalopods**.

■ **Monotremes**
Primitive egg-laying mammals. The platypus and echidnas are the only living representatives of this group.

■ **Mosasaurs**
Large marine **reptiles** that lived during the Cretaceous Period.

■ **Multituberculates**
Rodentlike mammals of the Late Jurassic to Paleogene Periods. All were very small.

■ **Myriapods**
A group of many-legged **arthropods** that includes centipedes and millipedes.

■ **Nautiloids**
Primitive **cephalopods** with thick shells. Only a single **genus** survives.

■ **Neognathae**
A group of birds that evolved during the Late Cretaceous. They include most flying birds plus swimming and diving birds such as modern penguins.

■ **Neornithes**
The **clade** of modern birds (and their common ancestor) that have feathers, a beak covered in horn, and a four-chambered heart.

■ **Nodosaurs**
A group of **quadrupedal ornithischian** armored **dinosaurs**.

■ **Nothosaurs**
Extinct marine **reptiles** with four paddlelike limbs that lived during the Triassic Period.

■ **Orbit**
The eye socket.

■ **Ornithischians**
"Bird-hipped" **dinosaurs**—one of the two main dinosaur groups. They were **herbivores** and had hooflike claws. See also **Saurischians**.

■ **Ornithodirans**
The **archosaur clade** that includes **dinosaurs**, their early ancestors the **lagosuchians**, and **pterosaurs**.

■ **Ornithomimids**
A group of **theropod dinosaurs** whose name means "bird-mimic." They outwardly resembled flightless birds.

■ **Ornithopods**
A group of **ornithischian dinosaurs** that have no hole in the outer, lower jaw and a long **pubis** that extends farther forward than the **ilium**. They were beaked, mostly **bipedal herbivores**.

■ **Ornithothoraces**
A **clade** of birds that had evolved the alula—a feather that directs air over the upper surface of the wing.

■ **Oviparous**
A term used to describe animals that hatch from eggs.

■ **Oviraptorosaurs**
A **clade** of feathered **maniraptoran theropods**, many of which were toothless, that included *Caudipteryx, Avimimus*, caenagnathids, and oviraptorids.

■ **Pachycephalosaurs**
A group of **bipedal ornithischian dinosaurs** with immensely thick skulls.

■ **Paleontology**
The branch of biology that studies the forms of life that existed in former geologic periods.

■ **Paleontologist**
A scientist who studies **paleontology**.

■ **Pangaea**
A supercontinent consisting of all of Earth's landmasses that formed at the end of the Paleozoic Era.

■ **Parareptile**
A group of extinct **amniotes** considered not to be true **reptiles**.

■ **Pareiasaurs**
A group of early **parareptiles** with massive, heavy bodies and stout limbs.

■ **Permineralization**
The process in which minerals are deposited within the fabric of a bony fossil.

■ **Perissodactyls**
A group of hoofed mammals that includes horses, rhinoceroses, and tapirs.

■ **Petrification**
The process by which organic tissue turns to stone.

■ **Phytosaurs**
A group of extinct semi-aquatic **archosaurs** superficially resembling crocodiles.

■ **Placentals**
Mammals whose unborn young are nourished by an organ called a placenta.

■ **Placoderms**
A class of jawed fish protected by armor plates.

■ **Placodonts**
Aquatic **reptiles** that lived in shallow seas during the Triassic, becoming extinct at the end of the period. Many had turtlelike shells.

■ **Plesiosaurs**
Large marine **reptiles** of the Mesozoic Era with pairs of flipper-shaped limbs.

■ **Pliosaurs**
Large, short-necked **plesiosaurs**.

■ **Predator**
An animal that preys on other animals for food.

■ **Prehensile**
Able to grasp something by wrapping around it. An animal with a prehensile tail is able to grasp branches with it, for example.

■ **Primitive**
Having characteristics similar to those of earlier forms.

■ **Proboscideans**
A group of mammals with trunks that includes modern elephants as well as the now-extinct mammoths.

■ **Procolophonids**
A group of early herbivorous **parareptiles** of the Triassic Period.

■ **Protozoans**
General term for single-celled animals.

■ **Psittacosaurs**
A group of **bipedal**, herbivorous **ceratopsians** with a parrotlike beak.

■ **Pterodactyloids**
Short-tailed **pterosaurs** that replaced earlier long-tailed forms.

■ **Pterosaurs**
Flying **archosaurs** closely related to the **dinosaurs**.

■ **Pubis**
A bone that is part of the pelvic girdle. It points downward and slightly toward the front in **saurischians** and downward and toward the tail in **ornithischians**.

■ **Pygostyle**
The short tailbone of a bird, formed from fused tail **vertebrae**.

■ **Quadrupedal**
Walking on four legs.
See also *Bipedal*.

■ **Radius**
One of the two lower arm bones.

■ **Ratites**
A group that includes most large flightless terrestrial birds, such as ostriches, emus, and their kin.

■ **Reptiles**
The common name for a group of animals characterized by having scales (or modified scales), being ectothermic, and laying eggs with shells. This is not a natural group as it does not include all of its descendants.
See also *Ectotherms*.

■ **Rhynchosaurs**
Herbivorous, land-dwelling **diapsid reptiles** from the Late Triassic Period.

■ **Robust**
Large form of a **species**.
See also *Gracile*.

■ **Sacrum**
The **vertebrae** of the lower back fused to the pelvis.

■ **Sarcopterygians**
A group of bony fish with fleshy fins, including lungfish, coelacanths, and many extinct forms. See also *Lobe-finned fish*.

■ **Saurischians**
"Lizard-hipped" dinosaurs—one of the two main **dinosaur** groups. Saurischians are divided into the **theropods** and **sauropodomorphs**.
See also *Ornithischians*.

■ **Sauropodomorphs**
Large, four-legged, long-necked herbivorous **saurischian dinosaurs**. They gave rise to the enormous **sauropods**.

■ **Sauropods**
Huge, **quadrupedal**, herbivorous **dinosaurs** with long necks, small heads, and long tails.

■ **Sauropterygians**
An group of extinct aquatic **reptiles** from the Mesozoic Era. They include **plesiosaurs**, **nothosaurs**, and **placodonts**.

■ **Sclerotic ring**
A ring of bones that supports the structure of the eye.

■ **Scute**
A bony plate with a horny outer covering embedded in the skin.

■ **Seed ferns**
Primitive seed plants (Pteridosperms) that grew in swampy areas through the Paleozoic and Mesozoic Eras.

■ **Sirenians**
A group of mammals that includes modern sea cows (manatees).

■ **Species**
In Linnaean classification, the level below a **genus**. Only individuals within the same species can breed and produce viable, fertile young.

■ **Stegosaurs**
Four-legged **ornithischian dinosaurs** with bony plates and/or spikes down the neck, back, and tail.

■ **Sternum**
The breastbone.

■ **Synapsids**
A group of **tetrapod vertebrates** distinguished by having a skull with a low opening behind the eyes. Synapsids include mammals and many other Permian and Triassic forms.

■ **Tarsal**
Ankle bone.

■ **Teleosts**
A group of advanced bony fish.

■ **Temnospondyls**
A group of early **tetrapods**.

■ **Tetanurans**
One of the major groups of **theropod dinosaurs**. The rear part of the tails of tetanurans were stiffened by interlocking bony ligaments on the **vertebrae**.

■ **Tethys Sea**
A shallow sea that existed during the early Mesozoic Era, separating the northern landmass of **Laurasia** from **Gondwana** in the south.

■ **Tetrapods**
Four-legged **vertebrates** and the vertebrates descended from them.

■ **Thalattosaurs**
Large, lizardlike marine **reptiles** that lived in the Triassic Period.

■ **Therapsids**
A general term used to describe **synapsids** in the Permian and Triassic Periods. This group includes mammals.

■ **Therizinosaurs**
A group of strange **theropod dinosaurs** that had a toothless beak and four toes on each foot.

■ **Theropods**
A suborder of **saurischian dinosaurs**. They were **bipedal** and mostly carnivores.

■ **Thyreophorans**
Armored, plated, and/or spiked **ornithischian dinosaurs**. They included the **ankylosaurs** and **stegosaurs**.

■ **Tibia**
The shin bone.

■ **Triconodonts**
An extinct group of small, early mammals that lived from the Triassic until the Cretaceous Period.

■ **Trilobites**
Early **arthropods** with external skeletons divided into three lobes.

■ **Troodontids**
A group of small, lightly built, long-legged **maniraptoran theropods** with unusually large **braincases**.

■ **Tyrannosaurids**
A family of very large **coelurosaur theropods** with two-fingered hands, small arms, a large head, sharp teeth, and powerful hind legs.

■ **Ulna**
One of the two bones of the lower arm.

■ **Ungulates**
Hoofed mammals such as horses.

■ **Vascular plants**
Land-living plants with a specialized system of tubes that carry water and nutrients.

■ **Vertebrae (sing. vertebra)**
The linked bones that form the backbone in **vertebrates**.

■ **Vertebrates**
Animals with a backbone and a skull made of bone or cartilage.

INDEX

ACKNOWLEDGEMENTS

Dorling Kindersley would like to thank Alison Woodhouse for proofreading the text and Jane Parker for compiling the index.

REVISED EDITION
For their help in preparing the revised edition Dorling Kindersley would like to thank:
Sue Butterworth for compiling the index; Anjali Sachar, Arshti Narang, and Debjyoti Mukherjee for design assistance; Ankita Gupta, Chhavi Nagpal, and Tina Jindal for editorial assistance; Deepak Negi for picture research assistance; and Suhita Dharamjit (Senior Jacket Designer), Rakesh Kumar (DTP Designer), Priyanka Sharma (Jackets Editorial Coordinator), and Saloni Singh (Managing Jackets Editor) for help with the jacket.

Smithsonian Enterprises:
Kealy Gordon, Product Development Manager
Jill Corcoran, Director, Licensed Publishing
Brigid Ferraro, Vice President, Consumer and Education Products
Carol LeBlanc, President

National Museum of Natural History: Matthew Miller, Collections Volunteer Manager, Department of Paleobiology

PICTURE CREDITS
The publisher would like to thank the following for their kind permission to reproduce their photographs:
(Abbreviations key: b=bottom, c=centre, l=left, r=right, t=top, b/g=background)

5: 123RF.com: Mark Turner (tr). Getty Images / iStock: Vac1 (br); **10:** Queensland Museum; **11:** Royal Tyrrell Museum, Canada (br, cr); **17:** Alamy Stock Photo: Sergey Krasovskiy / Stocktrek Images (fcra). Nobumichi Tamura / Stocktrek Images (cra). Dorling Kindersley: James Kuether (cr); **22/23:** Corbis /ML Sinibaldi; **24/25:** Corbis/Yann Arthus-Bertrand (b/g); **27:** Natural History Museum (cl); **29:** Dorling Kindersley: Natural History Museum, London (clb); **30/31:** Corbis/Michael & Patricia Fogden (b/g); **30:** Natural History Museum (cl); **31:** 123RF.com: Corey A Ford (crb). Dorling Kindersley: James Kuether (br); **32/33:** Getty Images/William J. Hebert (b/g); **34/35:** Corbis/Michael & Patricia Fogden (b, c). Getty Images/Harvey Lloyd (t); **36/37:** Getty Images/Harvey Lloyd (b/g); **36:** Getty Images / iStock: breckeni (br); **37:** Natural History Museum, London (br); **38:** Masato Hattori; **42:** Getty Images / iStock: Vac1 (cr, b); **43:** Dorling Kindersley: Institute of Geology and Palaeontology, Tubingen, Germany (b). Corbis (tr). Natural History Museum (tc); **48:** © cisiopurple / cisiopurple.deviantart.com: (t); **49:** Dorling Kindersley: James Kuether (cr). Getty Images / iStock: breckeni (b); **53:** Carnegie Museum of Art, Pittsburgh (cr); **55:** American Museum of Natural History (t). Yorkshire Museum (b); **57:** Masato Hattori (b). Natural History Museum, London (cr); **58:** Science Photo Library: Mark P. Witton (br); **58/59:** Corbis:/Michael & Patricia Fogden (b/g); **61:** Dorling Kindersley: James Kuether (tr); **62:** Science Photo Library (b); **64/65:** Dreamstime.com: Jeroen Bader (beach); **64:** Smithsonian Institution (br); **65:** State Museum of Nature (tc); **67:** 123RF.com: Corey A Ford (cb). Carnegie Museum of Art, Pittsburgh (br); **68/69:** 123RF.com: Tommaso Lizzul (b/g). Dorling Kindersley: James Kuether; **71:** Dorling Kindersley: James Kuether (cb). **76:** Carnegie Museum Of Art, Pittsburgh (cr); **77:** The Institute of Archaeology, Beijing (cr); **79:** American Museum of Natural History (t); **82:** Dorling Kindersley: James Kuether (b); **86/87:** Dreamstime.com: Jeffrey Holcombe (b/g); **87:** Royal Tyrrell Museum, Canada (b). Senekenberg Nature Museum (t); **88:** Royal Tyrrell Museum, Canada (c); **90/91** Dorling Kindersley: James Kuether (b); **97:** Hunterian Museum (**tr**). Natural History Museum, London (b, br); **99:** Natural History Museum, London (br); **101:** Science Photo Library: Mark P. Witton (t). Natural History Museum, London (br); **103:** Natural History Museum, London (br); **104/105:** Corbis (b/g); **105:** Alamy Stock Photo: Nobumichi Tamura / Stocktrek Images (cr); **107:** 123RF.com: Corey A Ford (br); **108:** © cisiopurple / cisiopurple. deviantart.com: (b); **110/111:** Dreamstime.com: Omdeaetb (b/g); **111:** Natural History Museum, London (c); **112/113:** Dreamstime. com: Pniesen (b/g); **113:** Senekenberg Nature Museum (tr); **114:** Dorling Kindersley: James Kuether (cra); **115:** Dorling Kindersley: James Kuether (br); **118:** Dorling Kindersley: James Kuether (b). American Museum of Natural History (tr); **119:** Dorling Kindersley: James Kuether; **120:** Dorling Kindersley: James Kuether (cr); **121:** Alamy Stock Photo: Emily Willoughby / Stocktrek Images (ca). Dorling Kindersley: Royal Tyrrell Museum of Palaeontology, Alberta, Canada (b). Alamy Stock Photo: Emily Willoughby / Stocktrek Images (ca). © cisiopurple / cisiopurple.deviantart.com: (b); **123:** © cisiopurple / cisiopurple.deviantart.com: (cra); **127:** 123RF.com: Michael Rosskothen (cra); **129:** Queensland Museum (t). Royal Tyrrell Museum, Canada (br, b); **131:** Natural History Museum, London (b). Witmer Laboratories (tr). Natural History Museum, London (cr); **133:** Royal Tyrrell Museum, Canada (c); **134:** Royal Tyrrell Museum, Canada (tr); **136:** Dorling Kindersley: James Kuether (br). Natural History Museum, London (tr); **138/139:** Getty Images (b/g); **138:** Royal Tyrrell Museum, Canada (tr); **139:** Natural History Museum, London (tr); **140:** American Museum of Natural History (tr); **141:** Natural History Museum, London (c). Science Photo Library (b); **142/143:** Dorling Kindersley: James Kuether. Dreamstime.com: Günter Albers (b/g); **143:** Natural History Museum, London (tr, cr); **144/145:** Dorling Kindersley: James Kuether (t); **145:** Photo of CRSL. Ligabue (tr); **147:** Smithsonian Institution (cr); **150/151:** Getty Images (b/g); **152/153:** Getty Images: Sergey Krasovskiy / Stocktrek Images (t); **152** Getty Images: Sergey Krasovskiy / Stocktrek Images (cl); **154:** 123RF.com: Mark Turner (cr); **157:** Alamy Stock Photo: Nobumichi Tamura / Stocktrek Images (ca); **158/159:** Corbis (b/g); **160/161:** Corbis (b/g); **163:** Natural History Museum, London (t); **164:** American Museum of Natural History (b); **167:** Natural History Museum, London (tr); **169:** Natural History Museum, London (tr); **170/171:** Dorling Kindersley: James Kuether (bc); **172:** Natural History Museum, London (c); **174/175:** Corbis (b/g); **174** Alamy Stock Photo: Sergey Krasovskiy / Stocktrek Images (bl); **177:** Willem van der Merwe: (cra); **178:** Corbis (b); **179:** Science Photo Library: Mauricio Anton (tr). Clemens v. Vogelsang: (cra); **180:** American Museum of Natural History (b); **184:** Natural History Museum, London (b); **185** Alamy Stock Photo: Sergey Krasovskiy / Stocktrek Images (b); **186** Science Photo Library: Jaime Chirinos (t). **188/189:** Corbis (b/g); **192:** Natural History Museum, London (tr); **192/193:** Dreamstime.com: Mathiasrhode (b/g); **194/195:** Corbis (b/g); **198:** Alamy Stock Photo: Natural History Museum, London (br); **199:** Natural History Museum, London (br).

All other images © Dorling Kindersley.
For further information, see www.dkimages.com